Dedication

To my parents, whose optimism, creativity, and unending love I owe everything.

To professor of philosophy Edwin B. Allaire, who suggested I write this book.

I Like to Run Too...

two decades of sitting

A memoir of growing up with a
physical disability

Stacy Zoern

Science & Humanities Press
PO Box 7151
Chesterfield, MO 63006-7151

Copyright Notice:

Graphics credits:
The cover is derived primarily from a painting by Barbara Zoern.
The photo of Stacy Zoern is by Diana Killian

ISBN 1-59630-017-5

Library of Congress Cataloging-in-Publication Data
Zoern, Stacy, 1979-
  I like to run too-- : / two decades of sitting : a memoir of
growing up with a physical disability / Stacy Zoern.
    p. cm.
  ISBN 978-1-59630-017-0 (alk. paper)
  1. Zoern, Stacy, 1979- 2. Women with disabilities--United
States--Biography. 3. Spinal muscular atrophy--United
States--Biography. I. Title.

HV1569.3.W65Z64 2007
362.4'3092--dc22
[B]   2006038797

Science & Humanities Press

PO Box 63006

Chesterfield MO 63006-7151

sciencehumanitiespress.com

Preface

Having a disability has meant a life filled with difficulties. It is almost every day that I face a new challenge, an obstacle, an ignorant, prejudiced person, a physical barrier, or an unjust situation having to do with my disability. On bad days, I encounter more than one of these. I always have a disability, every moment of every day, and it affects everything I do on some level. Whether I am following the ramped course to class on my college campus, deciding where to go for lunch, or just going around in public, where everyone always stares at me, my disability is in the back of my mind. I wrote the following because I want to share my experiences with people who have disabilities so they can relate, but also with people who have never had a disability or perhaps never even known anyone with one, so they can understand. Even if we, as human beings, were only to have a slight understanding of each other, our interactions would be exponentially more fruitful than if we were to remain submersed in ignorance. My roommate was at a party not long ago and was talking to a guy when I came up in the conversation. When she told him that she helped me and further, when the conversation led to the camp for children with disabilities that she volunteers at, he replied that she must be a good Samaritan, he could "never hang around handicapped people so much." I don't know who he is, or how widely those feelings reach across the population, but I have to do what I can to change that attitude. The other day someone was parked in front of the ramp at my dorm and I had to go all the way down the street to get up the curb. When I came back around, the girls who had blocked the ramp were just getting into their car. I went up to their window and told them that I had just gone all the way down the street because they had blocked the ramp, the ramp right next to the HUGE sign that says DO NOT BLOCK RAMP. They apologized and when I turned around, my parents, who were still across the street unloading the van, saw the girls start to laugh. Was something funny? Please God, do not tell me that is my place in this world. It is also important to me that I make something very clear to everyone reading about my life. The events that I talk about, despite what they may seem, are not unfortunate. Though I have wished at times to experience some of the things that I am missing, I have never regretted having a disability. Just like everything else about me, my disability has in part made me who I am. I think about the things that have happened in my life solely because of my disability, and I know that my life would be a completely different one if I spent it walking around. I wouldn't want a completely different life. Life is difficult and sometimes filled with tragedy. It is pointless to complain about the things that go "wrong" because the ideal picture of life that many people hold on to isn't really what life is at all. These "wrongs" are life. Though mine may be filled with a disability, it is also filled with love, ambition, and hope. What I hope for mostly is to help people see disability differently. Truthfully, I can't help but to smile about most of the obstacles I encounter. My family and I have spent many hours in hysterical laughter about the situations we find ourselves in. So, I suppose in a way, the things in my life that arise because of my disability are a form of entertainment. So be informed, be given a new perspective, and be entertained.

1

I came screaming into this world on November 23, 1979 when, after being stuffed by an enormous Thanksgiving dinner, my mom went into labor. She was only twenty years old, my father slightly older at 24, and I was their first. They were living in Fort Worth, Texas due to a bitter dislike of the brutally cold winters of Chicago, the only weather they had ever known, and an attempt to escape from familial dysfunction. They were alone, 1000 miles from the place of their youth, and they had an opportunity to make a fresh start with a family of their own. It was an exciting time in their lives.

After three agonizing hours of labor, without medication (it was technically still the seventies), the doctors delivered a healthy baby girl. All was where it should have been, I had ten fingers, ten toes, and no complications. For the longest nine months in a lifetime, while being pregnant, most women hope and pray that their unborn child is developing normally, and this desire without a means of validation can become consuming. There are a plethora of problems that can occur in chromosomes, genes, and genetic material during the development of a fetus. When I was born and the doctors declared that I was healthy, naturally it was a breath of fresh air for both of my parents. The second breath of fresh air occurred for my mother when I did not look like Raggedy Ann, a vision my mom had been having nightmares over due to my father's strawberry blond hair. I was now officially a citizen of the world, and on the third day I was sent home.

For many months my parents' days were filled with the joys of having a newborn; even when having a newborn included waking at three in the morning to stumble out of bed and into my room to console my agitation. This consolation consisted of the routine diaper change, rocking, or feeding of milk. I seemed to be developing like any normal baby; I was aware and interacting with my environment, especially when that meant laughing at the goofy faces people made while cooing over me. I began to hold my head up without support and soon began to sit. I also began to crawl which meant I began to get into trouble. My father once found me in the bathroom with a roll of toilet paper, unrolled, covering the area surrounding me...I had found yet another original way to entertain myself.

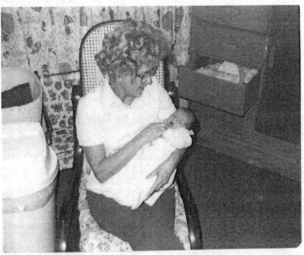

My pediatrician who saw me often for regular checkups during the first year did not notice any irregularities in my behavior or abilities. He would administer my immunizations, get me screaming, and send us on our way so my parents would have to be the ones to deal with my displeasure. But overall, I was a happy baby and my unsuspecting parents were learning as they went along, as first time parents have to do.

Over time however, my mom began to become concerned because I was not pulling up in my crib, nor even attempting to do so. As more time passed I was showing no interest in standing either. If held under the arms with my feet resting on the floor, my legs would just hang limply, not able to support my weight. It was my mother who was the one to notice this abnormality and it was she who first

mentioned the subject in the doctor's office. It was my first year checkup. As a result of my mother's concern and not by any awareness or insight on the doctor's behalf, he decided to perform a simple test. He laid me down on my back, lifted both of my legs into the air pointed toward the ceiling, and let go. My weak, heavy legs went crashing down to the table. As if hit by a bolt of lightning, a piercing terror cut into my mother, draining the life from her body...there was definitely a problem. The pediatrician had no ideas about what was wrong and only informed my mother that she would inevitably be taking me to many doctors from that point on.

My parents were in the process of being transferred to Houston about that time, so for several months the projects associated with a move to a new city prevented them from devoting all of their time to searching for answers. They didn't know what was causing my inability to stand and they didn't even know who could tell them. My mother, unsure of what she could do, bought expensive shoes for me thinking that just maybe with the right support for my ankles I would be able to stand. This proved to be a futile attempt. Nothing she could imagine doing in her wildest dreams was going to help me to walk; she was powerless. Confused, sickened, and without guidance, my parents found themselves resorting to a phone book for specialists. It was then that the doctor visits started. One appointment with a specialist was made after another, each behind a waiting list of months, and each resulting in a common conclusion, with doctors being unable to determine what the problem was.

The first doctor was an orthopedic surgeon who was searching for a malfunction in my bones. After numerous x-rays he found no such malfunction. He did recommend that we see a neurologist. Having not been recommended to anyone in particular, my parents randomly picked one.

Dr. Zeller, a neurologist, was contacted and again my parents waited. Finally he admitted me into a hospital in the Houston medical center for 10 days. He scheduled a series of tests for me including a spinal tap, a puncture made in the lumbar that can detect spinal cord and brain damage and some neurological disorders. Not surprisingly, this test did not detect any abnormality or lapomas, fatty tissue buildups on the spine that they thought might be causing the disorder in my legs. Dr. Zeller also performed an EMG, which entailed tiny needles being poked into the muscle tissue all over my body to measure muscle response. This too was inconclusive. Although the results indicated abnormal responses, no diagnosis could be made. At the end of the ten days, Dr. Zeller diagnosed me with "paresis of unknown etiology." In other words, he didn't know.

He then sent us to a brace company to have long leg braces made for me. Measurements were taken and then more time was spent waiting. The braces started at my tiny waist with an adjustable leather belt and metal strips that came down on both sides of my thighs to form a hinged knee and then continued down as metal strips that ended in two extremely small white leather baby shoes. These braces were to be used in conjunction with a metal walker. Sure the long leg braces allowed me to stand, they supported me enough for that, but they made the impossible task of walking an even greater impossibility. They were so heavy and awkward that the motion they did afford me was at best a waddle in slow motion...the braces and walker were not the answer.

My parents were young and lacking the support and knowledge necessary for such an emotionally exhausting experience. After another six months passed, my frustrated parents decided that not knowing what was wrong would not due, not only were the braces not working, but my

5

parents could not make an educated decision about having more children since they didn't know what my disorder was. Someone needed to give an explanation, a solution, a clarification...something.

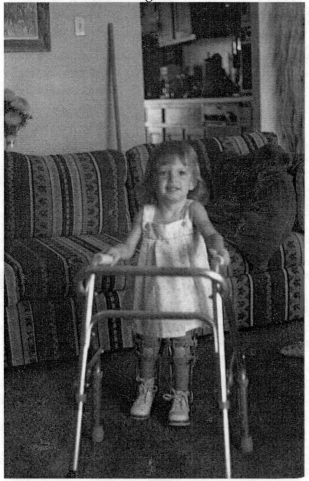

My grandfather on my father's side was a member of the Medinah Shrine Club and so had connections to Shriner's Hospital for Crippled Children, a selective hospital that also required an application. Many forms had to be filled out and pictures had to be sent of me wearing the long leg braces. At that point, what wouldn't my parents have done?

It was several months before I was accepted and my parents were allowed to make an appointment. This period was filled with anticipation, as was the day when we first met Dr. Butler.

Dr. Butler was the neurologist with whom we had been scheduled to meet. When we arrived at the clinic, there were many families there, and my parents had to wait patiently for my name to be called. We were finally called into a large, cold, sterile room that was filled with examining tables. My mom gingerly placed me on an examining table awaiting just another waste of time having had no questions answered. This time was different.

A cluster of doctors soon surrounded me, examining and discussing me with each other. After what seemed like hours, Dr. Butler stepped forward and spoke, revealing that he believed I had Muscular Dystrophy, but a muscle biopsy would be needed to confirm his diagnosis. A muscle biopsy was then performed on me, whereby a three inch incision was made on my upper left thigh and a piece of muscle was removed. It was then revealed that I had Spinal Muscular Atrophy, a form of Muscular Dystrophy. Everyone's worries were false, there wasn't anything wrong with my legs, there was something wrong with every muscle in my body.

This genetic disorder is caused from a naturally occurring chemical that for some reason kills motor neurons in the spinal cord of people with SMA. When these motor neurons do not communicate with the muscles, the muscles aren't used and therefore deteriorate making activities necessitating strength difficult if not impossible. A devastating conclusion for my parents, it meant I would never walk. If only that was all it meant...it meant I would never wash my own hair, it meant I would never put on my own jeans, it meant I would never get into bed without help, it meant I would never open a can of soup, it meant I would never ride a bike, it meant I would never lift a baby, it meant I would never stand tall and beautiful, it meant I would always have a disability.

Upon calling her mother for advice and some sort of reassurance and to tell her the news of my diagnosis, my grandmother proclaimed that my disease didn't run in the family and crudely suggested that my mother bring me up there...she would get me to walk. Her response was made from ignorance, but I suppose it was a legitimate ignorance. After all she was right, no one in the family had ever had the disease, in fact no one had even ever heard of it. And that went for my parents as well. Imagine being in your twenties, having what appeared to be a healthy first child, and then getting news like that.

What was to come as a result of this dreadful genetic disorder that my parents were unknowing carriers of? My parents knew looking at me at this state of innocence that life was only going to get much harder. I didn't even realize what was going on. Their visions of the future seemed quite bleak with the realizations that there would be no ballet classes and that my father would never walk me down the church aisle, arm in arm, on my wedding day. They had horrible thoughts about how I would be treated by other children; they feared ridicule and cruel behavior. Angered, they felt crushed, crushed by an uncaring God. How could He cripple an innocent baby? Maybe He didn't even exist. Needless to say a lot of questions were in their minds, seas of uncertainties that were quickly drowning any faith that previously existed. Their emotional state was unbearable; someone or something needed to be blamed.

2

The next few years were filled with days at the park feeding the ducks pieces of bread, lazy afternoons spent at the library checking out stacks of books, and just being a kid. Just being a kid for me turned out to be a lot like just being a kid for my parents too. If I wanted to play, which was basically during all of my waking hours, my parents were usually involved because I needed so much help. After trying Legos and realizing that I wasn't strong enough to push the pieces together, my parents resorted to buying me plain old blocks. I played for hours upon hours with those blocks. Like most children I went through a phase of being fascinated with living creatures and wanted something alive to put into my intricately created mazes. Since I couldn't do my own bug collecting, my dad would kindly round up the rollie pollies from outside for me.

I also loved Barbie and had more Barbie dolls than I could ever play with. Although I had the Barbie kitchen, the Barbie canopy bed, and dozens of other Barbie accessories, I found my time was most enjoyably spent dressing the dolls...over and over and over again. Those darn rubber legs though! I would become worn out and quite frustrated just trying to change her pants. I called my mom over to help me every few minutes. I think she grew to hate Barbie.

I was also intrigued by the sound of shoes on the floor. In elementary school, I would love to listen to the sound of people's shoes on the floor in the gymnasium. Any hard floor would do, and every shoe sounded different. I would have my parents position me on an edge of a chair in the kitchen so my feet would reach the floor despite my short legs, and there I would spend hours walking my legs, tapping my feet. As my feet hit the linoleum, I would imagine myself at school running down the halls or playing at recess.

In fourth grade, I took it a step further. I figured out that if I sat in my electric wheelchair, on the very edge, with my seatbelt loosened all the way, my feet could touch the floor. I could walk my feet as I drove my wheelchair, and it was just like I was walking around. I even went around school like that. I must have looked like the biggest weirdo. I even ran myself over once or twice. Luckily it was only a phase.

As an only child, I started asking my parents for a brother or sister. I didn't understand why we couldn't have a baby around who could grow to become a playmate for me. Little did I know that my mom had become pregnant and miscarried, probably a sign that no children were going to be escaping her womb without first being bitten by the fangs of a certain genetic monster.

10

In my parent's attempts to assuage my loneliness, they would buy me just about any doll that I became obsessed about as a result of the media. I would get up early in the morning, just as the sun was coming up, to sit on the living room floor and watch Saturday morning cartoons. Of course those target hours were filled with commercials to get children yearning for their products and begging their parents and Santa to come through for them. One particular fall, it was the Heather Doll who caught my eye. She was so real, she could even be fed food, and I knew having her would be just like having a baby sister. Unfortunately for my parents that particular baby sister was an expensive Christmas present at over one hundred dollars. Of course though, they couldn't let me down.

On Christmas morning as I eagerly tore open my presents, which was not an easy task, but one I wouldn't allow anyone to help me with (of course), I couldn't help noticing an unusually large package leaning up against the wall toward the back side of the Christmas tree. A present that was saved until last, my most anticipated gift had finally arrived. My dad opened the box and put batteries into my Heather doll whereby he then handed her over to me. My surge of excitement soon turned into a surge of disappointment; the doll was so heavy I couldn't even hold it, let alone manipulate it. That hundred dollars sat in the closet, practically unused.

Another Christmas my parents bought me an electric three-wheeler. This Strawberry Shortcake bike was a neat idea that ideally would have afforded me some freedom while playing outside. Only my foot wasn't strong enough to push down on the pedals and if one of my parents pushed it down for me, as they ran along next to the bike, I felt out of control and afraid of its motion. I had little balance and I thought I was going to fall off. I hated the bike.

Then there was the light bright whose bulbs I was not strong enough to push in; the marble tower whose pieces I was unable to assemble and whose top I couldn't even reach from my position on the floor to place the marbles at the beginning of their journey; and the chalkboard whose awkward size was not a good match for my weak arms.

Trick or treating was even difficult as a child. When I was very young, my parents would push me around, from door to door, but there were many houses that had steps leading to the front door. Although my dad could push my manual wheelchair up single steps, doing so was no longer possible when I got a heavy, electric wheelchair. The sidewalks leading to the front doors were often very narrow and bordered by plants. I was not able to get to those homes either. My parents and I had to cover five times the ground as most families just to fill my bag with candy.

As a child, my mother had no guidance or enthusiasm from her mother, and was never introduced to enriching, mind expanding activities. As my mother grew up seeing her friends in dance classes, ballet, music lessons, and gymnastics, she knew that if she ever had a daughter, her daughter would not miss out on such experiences.

To my mother's dismay, my cultured involvement in ballet and gymnastics would never be able to become a reality; however, with a creative approach and an open-minded instructor, I was able to take piano lessons. The piano was the ideal instrument for me; its functioning did not require any lung capacity, and its body rested on the floor, not in my weak arms.

While playing, I used the side of my hand to play an individual key, two fingers to play a single note, and I was unable to play chords. Although these may have been deviations from the norm, brought about by my frail fingers, I was able to play. I played for five years and performed in numerous recitals.

On the day of a recital, my mom would usually curl my long straight hair and tie it with ribbons. My mom would then put a dress on me, with tights, and dress shoes. The tights were so difficult to put on because I didn't have the strength in my legs to hold them down as she pulled the tights up. As she pulled up, my legs would just bounce up. My dad would usually have to help. Once we got to the place of the recital, I was always a little nervous, naturally I didn't want to make a mistake in front of my audience. The piano was usually up on a stage that could only be accessed by steps. Since I played from the piano bench, not my wheelchair, when it became my time to perform, my dad would carry me to the stage. It was imperative that when he lifted me he secured my dress underneath me. After all, I didn't want the entire audience to get a cheap thrill. As I was carried to the piano bench, everyone would just stare like we were at a freak show, not a piano recital. I despised being watched during that time and I wished I could have ordered everyone to avert their eyes. I simply wanted them to see me performing just like all of the other children.

When I was young, I was pushed around in a stroller or carried by my parents. This was probably the case for a little too long. I remember being at the grocery store, standing in line, my mom resting me on her hip, when a man jokingly said, "Don't you think you're a little too old to be carried around like that?" Little did he know that I couldn't walk and my mom carrying me seemed like the easiest thing to do at the time.

My first wheelchair, fitted to my small three year old body, and bright red for my three year old taste, brought with it a break for my parents' back and a sense of freedom for me. It was also a hard addition for my parents because with it came a realization on the next level of what my disability meant for all of us. The wheelchair was brought with us everywhere, neatly packed into the trunk, and unfolded for each use.

3

After a few years it was time for my mom to go back to work and it was necessary to find reliable child-care. The aspect of child-care was a nightmare throughout my baby-sitting years. Any mother is wary about who she leaves her child with and those feelings of uncertainty are only magnified when that child has a disability.

The first woman my mother called became very concerned when she heard that I couldn't walk. She politely indicated that she would not be able to baby-sit me because she and the children she watched liked to go to the library. My mom frustratingly informed her that we liked to go to the library too. She certainly was not the baby-sitter of choice.

A second baby-sitter agreed to care for me and so my mother began dropping me off in the mornings on her way to work and picking me up in the evenings. After several months of this routine, my mom was dropping me off one morning when the son of the baby-sitter cried out, "Mom, are we going to be taking Stacy over to Linda's house again so we can go swimming?" Apparently, this woman had been dropping me off at someone's house who my mother had never met, without my mother's knowledge, so her and the other children could go swimming...an activity which they obviously deemed me not to be worthy of participating in. That was the last day I stayed with her.

The next woman who baby-sat me was the first person that seemed to be another member of the human race. She cared for me for a long time and was trustworthy,

17

respectable, and honorable, all qualities which shone through when a mother of another child she baby-sat for told her that she had to stop watching me because she didn't want her child to "catch what Stacy has." The baby-sitter emphatically told her that she would not be able to stop watching me and so the lady removed her child instead. People. The complete and utter lack of knowledge about disability in the general public is amazing and sad.

What was sad was when a director of a daycare center complained to my mother that I had been sitting on the floor when someone brushed by me and I fell over, but did not even attempt to brace the fall. Imagine the audacity I must have had. The director was appalled and literally tattle told my behavior to my mother. My mother had to explain to the director that I have a disease that affects my strength (apparently she hadn't noticed my wheelchair). This happened to us at the same daycare center that gave me, a seven year old, an ultimatum.

We were to be going on our weekly field trip to the movies and then the park for lunch. The daycare director approached me in the morning and said that today I would not be allowed to take my small, fold-up manual wheelchair with me. So I could go on the fieldtrip without my wheelchair or stay at the daycare center with it. Some asinine reason was then given in an attempt to explain why I had to choose. All I knew was that she was an authority figure and I was very young and intimidated by her order. I also knew that a day without my wheelchair meant that I would have to have been carried in and out of the movie theater (an embarrassing and uncomfortable situation) and that I would be stranded sitting in one place, likely a park bench, while all the other kids ran around and played all afternoon at the park. I remember thinking how bored I would be, and more importantly, how left out I would feel when I would be sitting and watching the other children play while I was unable to participate. At seven years old I made the decision that my wheelchair, which gives me independence and essentially legs was more important than a day of "fun" because I like to run too...so I stayed at the daycare. For me the day was long and lonely and filled with thoughts about how badly I wished I was with my friends playing our imaginary games in the thicket of trees at the park. As can be imagined, my parents became slightly upset when I cried about the days events that evening. That was the last day I stayed at that daycare center.

Soon the obstacle of finding a baby-sitter to watch me all day wasn't an obstacle anymore because it was time for me to start school. A little yellow school bus came to my house on the first day of school, and I excitedly waved goodbye to my mom as the lift on the school bus raised me, and my wheelchair, inside. I was eager and very happy that I was going to be starting school. My mom, on the other hand, had to fight the tears as I was being taken away for the first time. My parents had no way of knowing how the other children would treat me at such a crucial time in the development of who I would become, what I would think of myself, and how I would perceive others' attitudes about me. I rode the little yellow school bus for the first time as I began kindergarten, and I might add that I rode it without fail until I graduated from high school, but that's another story for later. The interesting part about my riding the little yellow bus was not that it graciously picked me up at the end of my driveway whereby the driver would strap my wheelchair to the floor for safety, but rather that this bus was used for all the children with disabilities at my elementary school. The majority of these children had mental disabilities, ranging from mild retardation and Down Syndrome, to severe mental retardation. And here I was, a child with all of my mental faculties who was riding this bus because I couldn't climb the steps of a "normal" bus for the "normal" kids.

I had some horrific experiences over the years on those special education buses. One boy would pull on my hair when he could get a grip on it, or my shirt, and even once on my leg, a big deal considering that my legs don't straighten all the way and tendons can be easily torn in that manner. Those were all mildly painful experiences that the driver could do nothing to prevent since she was driving the bus while I was being beaten up. Everyday I would dread going to school for fear of what was to come. I began to hate riding the bus, and for reasons quite different from those that usually make children hate it.

Then there were the children who would vomit frequently and I would just pray it wouldn't reach me and then do all I could not to gag at the odor. One girl who rode my bus in high school would kick and punch and do everything she could not to get on the bus in the morning...so we would frequently be late to school. Unfortunately for me, I was the only person really affected by this delay because I was the only student who was in mainstream classes and so was missing important notes that would surely be on the next test. I was also the one who had to continually explain to my teacher why I was late to class.

One year, one of the students had seen my dog in the morning as I was getting on the bus. For the rest of the year, five days a week, two times a day, for thirty minutes each time, she would ask me what my dog's name was, over and over again. How many other students experience such elaborate interactions with people with cognitive disabilities on their bus ride to and from school everyday for 12 years?

There was also a boy who asked me everyday, in a new original way, if I would mess around with him. He was one of the many hormonally out of control boys on my bus that constantly harassed me. The main difference between him and all other high school boys was that his disability resulted in his inability to adhere to social norms. The physical and mental torments were never ending.

In elementary school I took the little yellow bus to school in my manual wheelchair. At first, the teacher would push me to lunch and recess, but all the children were intrigued by my wheelchair and would fight over turns to push me. My parents' worries were unwarranted, I never had any problems being teased or made fun of. My friends would push me around at recess and on many occasions would tip me over on the playground, an inevitable occurrence when running around on uneven grass. Like other kids though, I'd always go right back to playing around...after the teacher would run over in a panic and lift me and my wheelchair back up.

I gained some independence with the manual wheelchair in that I was no longer tied to an adult all the time, but I was still tied to someone because I was not strong enough to

21

push the wheelchair myself for very long. Brenda, the best baby-sitter who ever took care of me and who watched me for several years when I would get home from school, had a son Jason, who I would play with. One day we were outside playing and he was pushing me around when suddenly he lost control of my wheelchair while backing down a driveway. The scenario ended with me on my face in the street, my wheelchair practically on top of me, my lip busted, and my front teeth knocked loose. To this day, one of my front teeth is still darker than the rest due to nerve damage.

Although Jason and I would keep each other company when I was at Brenda's, over the years I had a few very close friends that I would spend time with at my house. Whether it was the girls in first and second grade, or my best friend later in elementary school, Stacey, (who I am still friends with) my parents had a lot of responsibility when it came to my social life.

Whether I wanted to spend the night with my friend, go to the movies, or be taken to the mall, my parents were almost always in charge. I was too much work and responsibility for any of my friends' parents to take on very often, and other parents rarely invited me along with them. Instead I was always inviting my friends over, and my parents were the ones who were constantly paying for my friend's movie tickets, chauffeuring me and my friends around, and making my friends dinner. My parents didn't really ever get a break. Over the years, our house was pretty much open to my friends all of the time…so much so that some of them even referred to my parents as mom and dad.

After several years of using a wheelchair my legs were noticeably contracted. As my parents had been informed of, children with SMA will never stand or fully straighten their legs for any amount of time and so the tendons behind the knees will contract.

One "solution" to this was a contraption that a physical therapist at my elementary school ordered for me. It had a base that stood on the ground, that was about 4 feet long and a foot or two wide, and it had two metal poles that came up the sides of the base. Connecting the poles were numerous thick, brown leather straps that could be tightened and stuck together with Velcro. My body was to stand between the straps. One strap went around my chest, another around my butt, another around my knees, and another around my ankles. The idea was that I could "stand" during my second grade class while all of my classmates sat, in order to straighten out my body. What no one thought of was how I would actually get in this thing. It's not like I could support my weight while they adjusted the straps, so it took several woman to balance and secure me. I am not exactly sure what the other children were doing while I was being manipulated in the back of the room. I have only one memory of this happening...I don't know if that means it was such a pain to put me in it that they gave up, or if I blocked the other instances out of my memory because it was so traumatic.

Another "solution" to my contracting knees was leg splints that I was to wear at night to stop the process. What a horrible and stupid idea. Sure, nobody wants their legs to get stuck in such a bent position that they have to sit on their calves, or so much that they can't put pants on...both consequences used as tactics to scare me into using the braces. But the degree to which the tendons will contract reflects the position the person has their legs in most of the time. For someone who can't walk, this is usually a sitting position. So maybe my knees are now stuck in little over a 90 degree position because I only wore leg splints at night for about two years. Well, all I can say is I sleep comfortably without metal on my legs and without my knees being stretched for so long at night that they hurt in the morning. Yes it's true my legs don't straighten all the way, but so what? It's not like I can walk anyway and I'd take a lifetime of real sleep over straight legs any day. It was terrible as a child to have to wear those leg splints and I'm sure it was just as terrible for my parents to have to put them on me and helplessly witness my discomfort...a common theme in their lives that was yet to unfold. Young children will always argue with their parents when they don't want to do something, whether it is to pick up their toys, or to eat their vegetables. I had to argue with my parents every night because I didn't want to wear the leg braces. For the short amount of time that we did use the splints, a marker was used to color on the velcro so that my progress could be recorded. The tendons did loosen as a result of the splints, but at an incredibly slow rate. Hardly worth the arguing and the tears.

When I was in third grade, the decision was made that it was time for me to get fitted for an electric wheelchair. My parents took me to a medical supply office where I was measured for my soon to be built, customized electric wheelchair. They had a used electric wheelchair there that didn't fit my small stature, but they agreed to let me drive it around in the parking lot so I could get a feel for what it would soon be like. They put me in it and then manually pushed it outside where they reconnected the battery and told me to go for it. For the first time in my life, at the age of nine, I experienced complete freedom, freedom from others, freedom from my own physical limitations, and freedom of my mind to make the decision to go wherever I wanted. As

I pulled away from my parents, alone, via my own will, they felt the surge of emotions likely similar to those of parents with children who are taking their first steps. My first steps were eight years past due.

The excitement I felt about getting my first electric wheelchair is indescribable. During the six months it took to build, I would imagine what it would be like at school, at home, at the mall, everywhere. Usually independence just happens for people during the natural progress of growing up, but mine was coming on a certain date, all at once, and I had six months to anticipate its arrival. What a long six months that was.

When my wheelchair was completed and I took it home for the first time, I was a disaster. Literally. The precision needed to control an electric wheelchair is an exact science because they are built to be extremely sensitive so someone with limited strength can move the joystick. The only problem, and one that fades with time, is that when one is learning how to master this precision, many walls, doorways, and furniture pieces are damaged. Little pieces of plaster on the floor near corners of the wall were common occurrences in our house. Sometimes my parents would hear the loud bang associated with my wheelchair colliding into a wall and when my dad came into the room to see what had happened, I knew I was in trouble. Most kids get yelled at for running in the house or throwing a ball near a window, I got yelled out for destroying the drywall. Luckily, my skill did improve, and before long I was getting on the lift of my little yellow bus in an electric wheelchair for the first time. Talk about freedom. School through my perspective completely changed. I was my own person, no longer an extension of the teacher or one of the students. The purchase of that highly technical piece of equipment was most definitely necessary for my personal growth.

Of course, the addition was popular with the students as well. It was no longer about who could push me, but rather who could touch my joystick causing me to thrust forward (a forbidden occurrence as far as I was concerned), or who could ride on my wheelchair by standing on the back wheely bars (a privilege I could have made a fortune from if only I'd had the sense to charge a nickel a ride).

The interest the students, especially the boys, had in my wheelchair continued all the way through high school. The guys were always asking me how fast my chair went, and inquiring about all kinds of technical information. I usually had no idea what they were talking about. There was one guy in high school who was in my study hall, but I didn't know him very well. He told me he wanted to ride in my wheelchair. I laughed and told him I thought that would be a little difficult since I was always sitting in it. He then suggested that I go to the bathroom, and while I was sitting on the toilet, he would take my wheelchair for a spin.

In elementary school, they weren't quite as bold, but they were certainly fascinated by the mechanics that went into my wheelchair. I was amazed too; my chair allowed me to move around and go anywhere I wanted. It *was* amazing. I would drive around on the playground with my electric wheelchair, over the grass and the never-ending bumps and couldn't believe my freedom. Sometimes I thought my wheelchair was so amazing, that I forgot I needed to be careful with it.

The first time that I realized that wasn't the case was in elementary school, when I spilled a carton of chocolate milk all over my joystick at lunch. I wiped it off right away, but it was too late. My wheelchair wouldn't work. Luckily, for reasons soon to be described, my manual wheelchair was at school too. My teacher put me in my manual wheelchair, and had my electric wheelchair lifted onto a dolly, where it sat at the front entrance of the school for the next few days.

When I would go to the front of the school it looked as if my wheelchair was on display. After some time had passed, I wanted to see if it was working. When we turned it on, it started right up, apparently it had dried out.

I also had to answer the frequent question among my peers, did the wheelchair belong to the school? Of all the questions to think to ask me, the only student in a wheelchair, it amused me that this one was so popular. Perhaps they thought if it wasn't mine then they had a chance of using it too.

I suppose their thinking that the wheelchair belonged to the school wasn't so far fetched, especially if they knew the system that was necessary for me to utilize my wheelchair at school. My parents both had to go to work for hours that long exceeded my 8:30 to 3:30 school days. We were living in Katy, a west suburb of Houston, and it was over an hour commute for each of my parents to get to work. Therefore, in elementary school, it was necessary for me to go to Brenda's house before and after school. The problem lay in how to get my very heavy, not collapsible electric wheelchair to Brenda's house in the mornings from my house and then back home again in the evenings. Although the bus with a lift took me from her home to school and back, there was not a way to transport the wheelchair from my house to Brenda's and back. We only owned two small cars, which only had capabilities of transporting a foldable manual wheelchair. The purchase of a van with a lift was not financially feasible for my parents at that time.

And, so it went for many years, I had my electric wheelchair at school, but at the end of the day I would be taken to the special education wing of the building where a special education teacher would transfer me to my manual wheelchair, plug in my electric wheelchair to be charged for the night, and push me out to get onto the bus. This meant that for many years I did not have my freedom in the afternoons after school at Brenda's, or in the evenings at home. The exceptions were Fridays when I would bring both wheelchairs back to Brenda's and my father and Brenda's husband, Lamar, would lift the massive wheelchair into the back of Lamar's pickup truck and Lamar would graciously drive fifteen minutes to bring it to my house so that I would not have to go the entire weekend without my legs.

My father soon acquired a mini-van as a work vehicle. This mini-van could fit my electric wheelchair behind the last seat if both of my parents strained their backs and lifted the 275 pound mass of metal. This difficult task was not a realistic option for every event as it was very awkward for their lower backs and could only be done on outings where they were both present. The result was simple, I too could have the independence taken for granted by most children and their parents, on special occasions. My parents didn't escape this limitation free either, since if I was lacking in independence it meant so were they...someone had to be pushing me around.

It was a real treat to be able to take my electric wheelchair to the mall. My mom and I loved to go shopping because it was one of the few things we could go out and do together. It was always a little frustrating though, because she would have to push me around. That meant that she had to push me through all the racks of clothing, she had to push me every time she saw something that she wanted to look at, and if I saw something I wanted to look at, she had to take me to it too. It was like we had one body for two brains.

Sometimes my dad would come with us and lift my electric wheelchair into the back of his van. This didn't happen very often though because not only does my dad hate to shop, it was very difficult to lift my wheelchair in and out of the van. He also had 75 boxes of work material

28

that he kept with him in the back of his van, and if I was to take my electric wheelchair, he had to unload every one of them and then load it all back again.

Though rare, the trips we did bring my wheelchair on were well worth the wait. My mom and I were able to experience shopping together as it was meant to be. Calling each other over to look at what we had found.

One particular special occasion I recall when I wanted my electric wheelchair was in fifth grade when there was a dance at the skating rink where everyone was going, including Jason, my crush. My parents recognized the importance of the event and so brought me in my electric wheelchair. The night was going great, and all the drama of the fifth grade girls trying to dance with the cute boys was ever present...my own drama included. All my friends knew I had a crush on Jason and so it was this big chain of gossipy girls going around spreading the word to ask him to dance with me. Somehow Robert, who was friends with Jason and who I also knew, got involved in my conquest for a dance. Then it happened, the rumor got back to me that Jason was going to dance with me. I was elated. However, my elation soon fizzled when I found out that it was to be at the price of a dollar, offered by Robert. I spent the rest of the night in the bathroom in tears. If I only knew then that the challenge in finding someone to dance with would resurface again and again, but would not always end so unhappily.

4

After much persuasion on my part, I finally convinced my mom that I was capable of coming home alone after school. This typical release of protection among parents is always a little scary, but was naturally more so for my parents. There was a lot I couldn't do for myself and a lot that could go wrong, but I *needed* to stop going to a baby-sitter after school. We got the particulars all worked out, I would carry the garage door opener to school with me (not a key like most kids because the only entrance with a ramp was through the garage), and the bus driver would walk to the door with me and open it. A fool proof system...and for the most part it was.

Except for the time that I somehow lost my balance and fell over so that my upper body was hanging down by my legs. I could feel the blood rushing to my head and it became hard to breath with the state of panic that was setting in. I absolutely could not muster enough strength to pull myself back up, but I knew I needed to do something because staying in that position for a few hours until my parents got home from work was not an option either. So I managed to get my hand on my joystick, drove over to a table, and used the table to knock my head up. Thank goodness I had the ingenuity to come up with the idea, but even more so that the table happened to be at just the right height for such a maneuver.

I was never very worried about anything happening that I couldn't handle. For the most part, if a problem arose, I would be able to find a solution. Sure, sometimes I would get very weak, like when trying to reach for something in

31

the pantry, but if I just sat still for a minute or two, I would regain my strength and success would be mine.

I also had a grabber that I could use to pick things up that I dropped. The grabber came in very handy, but could not be used to pick up everything since some things I could not get a grip on, or if I could, it was too heavy for me to lift anyway.

Sometimes, I dropped my grabber. We had a meter stick in the kitchen pantry, and sometimes I could lift my grabber up by sliding the meter stick in its handle. There were also several occasions when I dropped paper, and I would get the meter stick, put tape on the end of it, and get whatever I had dropped by sticking it to the tape.

One afternoon, I had just finished my Spanish homework, which included cutting and gluing a bunch of pieces together, when I dropped it. It fell way under my desk, and I couldn't get at it with my grabber. It wasn't a big deal, I had already finished it, and I would just have my parents pick it up for me when they got home. When they got home though, hours later, I had forgotten all about it. In fact, I completely forgot about it until the next day when the teacher told us to turn in our homework. After class, I went to my teacher and told her what had happened. I asked her if I could bring it in the next day. She told me she would not accept it late, not even for a few points off, and instead she gave me a zero.

Then there was the time that for some stupid reason I went outside, and on my way back in, got stuck over the hump in the door's entrance. I spent 45 short minutes there until my dad got back from work...lucky for me he got home early that day.

It wasn't as if my getting stuck had everything to do with the fact that I was home alone though. I had a friend who lived a few blocks away and I would go over to her house a lot. One Saturday morning I was on my way to her house and was just rounding the curve in front of my house where our corner cul-de-sac sidewalk became one with the main street sidewalk. I hit a bump that must have been the icing on the cake to an already loose wire and suddenly everything stopped. I was hopelessly stuck. After sitting for a few minutes I thought it would be beneficial to start screaming for help. Apparently I don't have a very loud voice. Once again, my father came to the rescue when he found me while he was getting the morning paper.

I have had an unwelcome awareness of the fallibility of my wheelchair as a piece of machinery since that day. It is pretty reliable, but not foolproof. After that day, when I would get home from school, alone, my first stop would be to get the cordless phone and put it in my lap. This security blanket allowed me to go about my business while knowing in the back of my mind that if my wheelchair started freaking out, I would be able to call for help.

5

There was a time when I was stronger, or more likely I was just younger and so weighed less, that I could crawl around on the floor. I even remember being able to pull myself, with a bit of effort, from a laying position to a sitting position. If in a kneeling position, I could walk on my knees next to the coffee table while holding onto its edge for support. I was definitely more flexible when I was younger because I hadn't been sitting all day every day for very many years yet, which has a powerful stiffening effect on one's body. The bigger problem when I was younger was that my feet were very sensitive from not being walked on. That hasn't changed, but it was more of an issue when I was younger and was being picked up from and put down on the floor. If any of my body weight was put down on my feet, they would be crushed and I would be in pain for weeks. Sometimes just the act of putting my shoes on would hurt them. Not to mention that when they were already hurt, it was practically impossible to put shoes on at all. It wasn't just getting on and off the floor though that put my feet in vulnerable positions, it was any movement where I was being picked up by the underarms and my legs were left free to dangle...and to get sat on. The result was that for many years I went around with the pain associated with a sprained ankle or similar injury.

As I got older, and bigger, lifting me in that fashion wasn't realistic anymore anyway, and the new lift incorporated support for my legs. This meant that my feet stopped getting injured. I still have a recurring dream that someone is trying to put me on the toilet and every time they lower me down, my feet start to go into the toilet instead of resting in front of it, so they lift me up and try to put me down again, but my feet keep going in the toilet.

The dream likely developed from my fear of sitting on my feet. After hurting them enough times, I would hold my breath in nervous anticipation every time someone was sitting me down. Even after I was being lifted in the new way that protected my feet much more, accidents would happen.

One evening my parents were going to drop my friend and I off at the movie theater where we were going to meet some other friends. My dad had even unloaded his van so I could take my electric wheelchair. Even though they would be lifting my wheelchair into the back of the van, I still had to be lifted from my wheelchair to the seat in the car since I could not sit in my wheelchair in the mini-van. I was getting older, and bigger, and it was getting more and more difficult for my mom to lift me, especially the awkward lift into the car. When my mom put me in the van, I was on the edge of the seat, and before she was able to move me back farther on the seat, I slid down and fell on my feet. I was in so much pain, I didn't even get to go to the movies that night.

The feet issue did indeed waiver as I got older, but my family and I had new issues to deal with. Serious issues. About the time we started the process of getting an electric wheelchair, I was diagnosed with Scoliosis. This curvature of the spine is very common, if not common to all, children with SMA. As I was getting older, and taller, the muscles around my spine were becoming less and less capable of holding it up. This process, if unheeded, will eventually cause the spine to curve until it crushes the internal organs and results in death. The fortunate part of the diagnosis was that there was something that could be done for Scoliosis so that death by it would not be inevitable. The

36

unfortunate part was that the something included two back surgeries and those back surgeries could not be performed until my spine was full grown, or at about age 12. The additional disclaimer was that the curving of my spine needed to be slowed in the meantime so that I would be able to make it that long. And so I was fitted for my first body brace.

This procedure which was done every six months for the next 4 years included being stripped naked and put on a stool with a noose-like object around my neck that was used to pull my spine as straight as possible while they wrapped cold, wet plaster around my body; a shameful process that not only resulted in my being physically naked, but also stripped me of all pride. Much like when having a cast made for a broken bone, I would then have to sit in that horrendous position until the plaster hardened and could then be cut from my body. The product of this agony was a brace that extended from my collarbone to its longest part, in the back, at my butt. It was fastened to me by a series of velcro strips and was worn under my clothes. The process of making the brace only got worse, and more painful, as I began to develop breasts. The plaster had to fit my body tightly to make the brace effective, and so this man who made the braces and who was a stranger to me, pulled the strips around me and forcefully patted them down onto my skin, including the tender skin on my chest.

The act of wearing the brace was always miserable. Living near Houston, it was terribly hot for a majority of the year. The undershirts I wore for a layer between the brace and my skin would be soaked with sweat during the summers. I longed to take the brace off in the evenings. For years I had to wear it without fail, and the degree of my curvature still increased by quite a bit...I don't even want to think about what would have happened had I not worn it.

As the time for my surgery grew nearer, and the curvature of my spine was at its greatest, I could hardly even tolerate sitting for any amount of time without my body brace on. Logically, there was one time when I couldn't wear it, when I took a shower. I had attained a bath bench when it became too difficult to lift me in and out of the bathtub. The bath bench certainly made life easier, but in the late stages of my Scoliosis, I could barely sit on it while my mom washed my hair. The mere pressure on my head pushing down on my unsupported spine was very uncomfortable. Taking a shower was no longer about playing with my toys in the bathtub until my skin became wrinkled like a raisin, or soaking in the bubbles, or even just enjoying the soothing feeling of hot water running down my body. Instead, taking a shower became about taking a shower as fast as I possibly could because it meant so much discomfort for me.

Part of my growing up with a visible, physical disability was a heightened sense of needing to feel normal. Perhaps because I couldn't do anything about the fact that I couldn't walk and used a wheelchair presupposed my accepting it. This may be why I did everything in my power to appear "normal" in every other way, because that I *could* alter and didn't have to accept, at least in my mind. I wonder if this will ever change.

The first thing I remember being ashamed of, wanting to hide for my fear of appearing less normal than I already appeared, was the scar on my thigh from the muscle biopsy. There was a point when I was in elementary school when I wouldn't wear shorts that revealed my scar. Although I got over that, it was replaced by something new...my body brace. Only my friends knew that I wore it and I wanted to keep it that way.

One year, in an attempt to give me some relief from the summer heat, they made my brace with a heart shaped cutout in the stomach. I was at school one day when Mario, a male acquaintance of mine, was kidding around with me and poked me in the stomach and walked away. I breathed a sigh of relief that he just happened to poke me where the heart cutout was and where he felt my soft stomach. I'm sure he would have been shocked had he felt something as hard as a rock, and I certainly would have been embarrassed.

Although I felt embarrassed about some aspects of my "abnormalities", I also found myself defending them. I had a friend named Tiffany in junior high that I was starting to spend quite a bit of time with. She lived in walking distance from my house, and we would play together after school and on the weekends. Her mom was very welcoming and willing to make the effort so that I could go with Tiffany and her family on outings. They would lift me into their car and then put my manual wheelchair in the back. I went shopping with them several times, and out to eat a few times too. After we had been friends for several months, Tiffany actually told me that her mother warned her she didn't want her getting too close to me because I was going to die soon. Not only did someone with no knowledge about my disability tell her 12 year old daughter that I was going to die, but Tiffany relayed that information to me!! I had an argument with her for an hour about whether I was going to die soon or not.

This was the same girl that disconnected my wheelchair against my will. My electric wheelchair had two levers that could be switched to disconnect my power and allow the wheelchair to be pushed manually. This was important so that if my wheelchair malfunctioned, I could still be pushed, and I would not be trapped. One day Tiffany and I were at my house alone and were having a disagreement. She wanted to do one thing and I wanted to do another, so by means of unplugging me she intended to limit my possibilities and force me to do what she wanted. I was appalled, angry, and rather frightened. I was sitting in the kitchen, unable to move, and she began to pull out pots and pans so she could bake brownies. She wasn't a very good kidnapper though because when I demanded that she give me the phone so I could call my mom, she did it right away. Of course my mom who was an hour away at work couldn't do much about the situation I found myself in. I used my heightened persuasive ability (developed fully from being a spoiled only child) and convinced Tiffany to reconnect my battery.

6

MDA camp was a better place to make friends if you wanted to be sure they wouldn't tamper with your equipment. The Muscular Dystrophy Association is a wonderful organization that offers emotional and financial support to people affected by a neuromuscular disease, not to mention providing a network to acquire information about Muscular Dystrophy. One of the many ways in which they support both people with Muscular Dystrophy and their families is MDA camp, held for one week each summer. I started going when I was six and haven't missed a summer. The privilege ends when I turn 22.

Basically, children aged 6-21 who have some form of Muscular Dystrophy are invited to go to a week long camp, free of cost. Volunteers, usually high school and college students, act as their caregivers, parents, legs, and friends. Not only has it given me the opportunity to meet people who share similar freaky stories and experiences with me a result of Muscular Dystrophy, but I have met some of my best friends for life in people who have volunteered their time there. Many people volunteer for years allowing deep bonds to form between campers and volunteers.

When everyone is the same, a bunch of wheelchairs rolling around, people are seen as who they are...people, not people in wheelchairs. The part of your identity revolving around your wheelchair is sort of lost because it is part of everyone's identity and so gets cancelled out and forgotten about. It certainly isn't what makes you different from everyone, not for a week. I guess that is why I have met such wonderful people there, because not only are they already above average for having volunteered a whole week of their time to intimately help someone, but they see who I really am because having everyone in wheelchairs doesn't only help the people in them feel more normal, it stops the attendants from seeing the wheelchairs too.

Sometimes it has been difficult to be seen for who I am, and this was certainly the case when I interacted with the public school system...from my earliest memories until I graduated from high school. The classifications and generalizations that were always being made about me were almost more than I could handle. As early as elementary school, it was clear to me that in many ways the school system did not know how to "deal" with me.

Although I seemed to have a bladder of steel in elementary school and rarely used the restroom, there were a few times when I did need to use the restroom at school. One of these times I guess the nurse didn't really know how to help me so she requested assistance from someone else. There apparently wasn't enough room for the three of us to maneuver in the restroom, because in order to pull my pants back on they had to step out of the restroom and into the nurses' office. Not only did they take me out of the restroom with my pants down, there was a little boy in the nurse's office. A little boy who saw more than I would have liked him to.

In my first few years of elementary school, the school was providing physical and occupational therapy for me. This finally ended when they decided nothing more could be done for me. Until they came to this conclusion though, a part of my therapy included getting on a school bus and going over to a local high school to go swimming in their pool. I would be taken out of my class to be tortured in a freezing cold, indoor swimming pool. I was so little, and the cold got to me so badly that I couldn't even function in the water, making it impossible to get any therapy done anyway. Not to mention that we would use one of the student locker rooms to dress, and although there were never masses of people in there, it was never empty either. The older girls intimidated me and I was worried about dressing in there with the thought that someone may come in.

The other student who was receiving therapy was a little boy who had been hit by a car while running into the street for a ball. He could not walk or speak due to his accident. I know they weren't going out of their way to protect his modesty either, since even I saw them changing his diaper once...a confusing and traumatic thing to witness. At such a young age I felt awkward seeing that he, a child my own age, wore a diaper. His intellect had not been affected by the accident and so I am sure he appreciated their flippancy too, although he could not communicate it.

Teachers were usually understanding about my disability and there were only a few things that made my disability awkward for them and myself. One of these was the disaster drill. In addition to fire drills, in elementary school we had disaster drills whereby a different alarm would come over the loud speaker signaling everyone to form a line up against the wall in a crouched position. The first time they had one of these, I was wearing a skirt, and in the teacher's attempt to get me on the floor, I flashed many of my classmates. Once on the floor, I wasn't able to sit in the "safe" position anyway. In future drills I always just sat in my wheelchair in a normal position. I guess the teachers weren't too concerned about the threat of a bomb or tornado occurring. I guess neither was I.

Once every year the whole elementary school gathered for field day. All day long all of the kids would participate in numerous athletic competitions from foot races to egg tosses. And every year, I would sit outside doing pretty much nothing all day. Although it was a nice diversion from being cooped up all day inside, it was still pretty boring. The worst part though was when we would all gather in the gymnasium at the end of the day for the awards to be given out. Without fail, every single year, the P.E. teachers would wait until all of the awards had been given out and then call my name and present me with a blue ribbon. The reasons for the award varied from year to year, but it didn't matter...I knew I had been sitting there doing nothing all day, everyone else knew I had been sitting there doing nothing all day...in short, it made me feel like an ass.

The P.E. program was a little backward though as far as I was concerned. For a couple of years I was a part of gym class with the rest of my grade level. Although I was exempt from the warm-up exercises that consisted of jumping jacks and sit-ups, they pretty much found a way for me to participate in the other activities. There were the square scooters on four small wheels that were used in some of the "sports." The gym teachers would put me on a scooter, although they had no support of any kind. Sometimes I would fall off. They also had some games that involved running around. Sometimes my wheelchair would tip over. My mom had to fight to get them to agree to let me do something a little more constructive with my time than banging my head against the gymnasium floor. This resulted in my having an unsupervised free period everyday. I would literally wander the halls, go see teachers I liked, and sometimes help them with grading or whatever they needed. I enjoyed being given responsibility and having trust ensued upon me to do as I pleased. I also befriended several teachers during my free time.

After several years of being exempt from P.E., I went into the gym with a friend to retrieve something she had left in the locker room. At first I wasn't even sure if I was allowed in there, like I would get in trouble for being somewhere I didn't belong. After entering the room, I felt very out of place and awkward. I was almost in awe of this "forbidden" place, and felt a sense of reverie for my friend who felt so at home there. My skewed perspective was not a result of my youth either, because my best friend in high school, Lauren, was in the drill team, and I remember feeling a similar way when I went with her once into her locker room.

The absence of any locker room experiences also left me feeling shyer about my body than other girls. I was always embarrassed changing in front of other people, and I noticed that others felt more comfortable with it. I did finally get over my shyness though, after living in a dorm room in college. I think I finally realized that few people (no one I have ever known) have the perfect Barbie doll body. Just because I don't have a perfect body doesn't mean I have to hide it.

7

I was always classified as being in special education because I needed the special transportation that was available to those students. Unfortunately, the generalizations that went along with being in special education were enough to cause a headache. I had to go through every test and evaluation regularly given to special education students until I graduated from high school. The problem I had with this was that most of the other children in special education had many more special needs than I did, the major distinguishing factor being that my disability did not affect my mind. The tests and evaluations always pertained to mental disabilities. For purposes of the school district though, it didn't matter. As far as they were concerned, we were all disabled and so had the same needs.

I had to take a test every few years to prove to them that I was progressing as I should be. One would think that knowing my diagnosis and knowing that Spinal Muscular Atrophy does not affect intelligence, that I would have been exempt from those insulting tests. If not, one would at least think that after the first one, or maybe even two tests that showed I was well above average as far as my intellectual ability was concerned, that they would realize the tests were no longer necessary. That wasn't the case either. Not to mention it was an oxymoron to have those tests administered to me, being that my second grade teacher had me tested for the gifted and talented program, to which I was accepted and remained a part of throughout my public schooling experience. They had to have known that I was above average for my age intellectually. Nonetheless, I was pulled away from my normal curriculum every few years, well into high school, in fact I was even pulled out of my honors geometry class once, to take these tests.

The reason I say the tests were insulting is because even the high school formatted tests included picking out shapes that didn't belong in a sequence, pointing out which sides of shapes were missing, and picking out patterns. These examinations lasted for hours and put me under a great deal of pressure. Although they were very simple and far under my level, I would become very stressed knowing that I would appear to be an idiot if I did not perform well. Also since the questions were so easy and my knowledge surpassed what they were searching for, I found myself thinking too hard and deeply over easy concepts. They were at what was for me an elementary level and so essentially I was being asked to think at a level that I was no longer at. To this day, I do not understand why I was subjected to such treatment. Would it have been so difficult to somehow classify me as having a physical disability and admit that such tests were disrespectful to my integrity?

The tests were not the only insults to my intelligence. Every few months, we would receive letters from the school district, including forms that needed to be filled out and returned. My mom would open a letter from the school and I just knew it was something ridiculous. The letters were always informative, telling my parents crucial facts such as that I would be graduating from high school and needed to have a plan for the future. Then we would have to fill out the forms asking whether or not I was aware that I would be graduating, whether or not I knew what that meant, and whether or not I knew I would need to get a job. I flat out refused to answer such questions. The people in the office who were responsible for sending the letters knew me personally, and it infuriated me that they even sent me such forms.

The forms and letters were actually just parts of the overall evaluations that would be done on me at the end of each year at the Admission Review and Dismissal (ARD) meetings. These meetings were when the principle and/or school counselor and my special education representative would sit down with my parents to discuss my progress. My parents would have to ask to get off from work and then drive from Houston where they worked back to Katy, where we lived and where I went to school, in order to sit in a meeting that was a complete waste of everyone's time. Most of the questions and topics did not apply to me since the only service I required was special transportation. So the time was spent telling my parents what they already knew, that I performed above average on tests of intelligence and that I was getting along well in school. These meetings, though not needed, were mandated by the state. If I had been able to have the luxury of a mother who didn't work and instead provided my transportation so that I never had to ride the special education bus, thus not requiring any services of the special education program, would I have ever been subjected to such tests, forms, letters, and meetings? Should the state require such things of students who use a wheelchair because of a physical disability? Are those useful ways of spending such precious state and federal resources?

Perhaps these evaluations put my teachers at ease. I certainly had a teacher or two who did not see me for who I was, but rather as the student in the class with a disability. In high school, I left my classes five minutes early so that I would have time to go to my locker and get to my next class before the bell released the crowds into the halls. I went to a 5A high school, which basically means it was huge. Between classes there were at least 2,000 students in the halls, some standing around in groups talking, some goofing around, others stepping over each other to get at their lockers. It was very difficult to maneuver between a

49

bunch of obnoxious high school students who were never paying attention and who were always falling over me and who would sometimes get run over. A friend would always leave early with me to help me open my locker and get my books for the next class, a task I was not strong enough to handle on my own. Though technically, these friends were offering a service to me, they were all eager to help as it meant getting out of five minutes of boring, torturous class time. My geometry teacher my freshman year of high school actually nominated a friend of mine for student of the year for helping me everyday, and she won the award. Good for her. After all, I am just a charity case, a pathetic gimp who has no friends willing to help without having to be paid off or rewarded. Nice.

I was also very disappointed in a teacher who I had known since elementary school. I first met Mr. Henry when, during one of my afternoons spent wandering the halls while my classmates were at physical education, his class was in the library watching a movie, eating candy, and he offered me a piece. When I got to fifth grade, he was my teacher, and I was very excited to have him since I had known him for so long. In addition to being a fifth grade teacher, he was also the sponsor for the Young Astronauts Club.

Membership to this club was a privilege earned by students with high grades. I remember when the announcement was made. We were all gathered in the school cafeteria, and someone was standing by the stage, calling each new member to the front, and I patiently waited to hear my name called. I wanted to be a member very badly. At last, my name was called, I had done it.

The year was filled with exciting field trips to NASA, and all kinds of fun activities, not to mention that we each got a blue jacket to wear, indicating our membership. The next year I moved on to junior high school, and I was in the first class to go through the newly built school. Mr. Henry was also one of the teachers who found a job at the new junior high, and so made the transition with us. Once again, the Young Astronauts Club, this time the junior high version, was accepting new members. And once again, I was invited to participate. There was a slight difference this time, one that would prevent me from joining a second time.

There were mandatory weekly meetings that members needed to attend if they were to be a part of the club. These weekly meetings were to be held after school, and this presented a huge problem for me. I had to take the bus home, it was the only way to transport my wheelchair. My family still could not afford to buy a van with a lift, and I couldn't exactly carpool like other children whose parents worked. What mom can get me and my electric wheelchair home because she has a van with a lift? Oh wait, there aren't any. My mom called Mr. Henry and explained our awkward transportation situation and told him that it would be a shame for me to miss out on such an earned privilege because of my disability. He told my mom that he would try to work something out, but he never did. I was very disappointed that Mr. Henry failed me. I was not a part of the Young Astronauts Club that year, or ever again.

During sixth grade, and from that time on, I used the bathroom at school once during the day. The school nurse, Mrs. Hunsucker, helped me use the restroom. Mrs. Hunsucker and I became good friends; I suppose a lot of bonding can happen over the toilet. There was a large, accessible restroom in the nurse's office, and that is the one that we would customarily use. There were times though, when Mrs. Hunsucker was especially busy at the time I came in to use the restroom, so she would send me over to the special education room to have those teachers help me instead. If only she had known how much I hated going

51

over there. I couldn't tell her though, I knew it would have sounded horrible and she probably wouldn't have understood. The special education room was entered through a door off of the main hallway; very visible. I must have been very insecure, or the junior high kids very relentless, or more likely a combination of both, because I used to hope no one would see me coming in or out of that room. I would even pass the room instead of going in if there were a lot of people in the hall. I was terribly embarrassed, even ashamed. I guess I was just afraid that someone who didn't know me very well would assume things about me or see me as less normal if they associated me with the mentally retarded children that were behind that door. I knew they would wonder what I was doing in there, and make assumptions about my abilities and my needs.

The whole bathroom at school scenario only got worse when I started my period. I had gone to bed one school night and felt terrible cramps in my stomach, but didn't consider what that could have meant. We were living in a fairly small, very inaccessible house at the time. When my parents had originally moved in, they still did not know I had a disability that would necessitate my using a wheelchair, and so they weren't considering the house's accessibility when they purchased it. I could not even fit my wheelchair into the bathroom. Not only was the door not wide enough, even if I had been able to fit through the doorway, there would have been nowhere to go, it was that small. Using the restroom at home involved one of my parents carrying me into the bathroom where they would sit me on the counter. They would pull down my pants there and then transfer me to the toilet. As I grew older, this became difficult and we would pull my pants down when I was sitting in my wheelchair, and then just carry me straight to the toilet from out in the hallway.

When I was younger I would sit on the counter to brush my teeth and wash my face too, but as I became older and heavier, this too was very difficult. I began to brush my teeth in the kitchen, with my wheelchair parked parallel to the sink. It wasn't easy and it was gross to spit in the kitchen sink.

When I started my period, my dad was the first one to notice since he, not I, was the person who dressed me in the mornings. He removed my bloody panties and being that it was an awkward situation for him, went to get my mother. Meanwhile I was in the bathroom, unsure of what was going on. My mom came into the bathroom and told me that I had started my period, the beginning of what would be a hellish experience.

I wasn't strong enough to insert a tampon myself so I had to use pads instead. Those weren't too easy either. Imagine sitting in a chair naked, and then trying to pull up a pair of panties with a thick pad on them, all without lifting your body up. Invariably, the pad would not go on right, it would get stuck to me, or roll up, but whatever would happen, I wasn't comfortable very often.

The blood was also a mess. Since I was sitting all day, the blood would pool inside of me, in pockets of my uterus. When I was lifted up to go to the toilet, the blood, having been unmoving for hours, would pour out, literally. At school, Mrs. Hunsucker would lift me from my wheelchair and carry me to the toilet, and I would leave a trail of blood on the floor. I would then have to watch her wipe it up, since I couldn't even clean up my own mess. We thought about pulling down my pants when I was on the toilet, instead of on my chair, but I leaned from side to side on the armrests of my wheelchair to help get my clothes on and off, and I would have had nothing to lean on if sitting on the toilet.

Naturally, Mrs. Hunsucker wanted to wear rubber gloves when helping me when I was on my period. I used to be so embarrassed though if students were in the nurse's office and saw us going into the bathroom together while she was putting on gloves. It made me feel so, I don't know. Not normal I guess. What would they think she was doing for me in there? I can wipe myself and didn't want anyone thinking otherwise!

Mrs. Hunsucker would get blood on her gloves while trying to adjust my pad and then sometimes she would get blood on the outside of my pants from her bloody gloves. I would then have to go around for the rest of the day with blood stains on my pants. My underwear also used to become very bloody because they were dragged underneath me when being pulled off.

One day, I was a bloody mess and I had a breakdown. I was sitting on the toilet, blood everywhere, on the floor, on my underwear, on my clothes, and I started bawling. We had paged my dad and he came to school, bringing me some fresh underwear. I felt as if I had no dignity. Nothing was private for me, not even the most private. There I was in the school nurse's office in sixth grade, sitting bloody on the toilet, my dad and the nurse in the restroom with me, tears streaming down my face.

Finally we just learned to take a brown paper sack with a few extra pairs of underwear to school for when I bled all over mine. I brought about three at a time, and I remember the days when it was time to bring the sack of dirty underwear home. I didn't use a backpack, because I wasn't strong enough to get my books in and out anyway, and so I had nothing to hide the bag of dirty underwear in. I just desperately hoped that none of the obnoxious boys I knew would see me on the way out to the bus and ask me what was in the bag.

Having a period was a miserable experience for me and the people who had to help me use the restroom. It was a mess and a pain in the ass. My mom was talking to my Aunt Paula, my dad's younger sister, on the phone one day and told her what we were going through. She suggested that I just wear diapers when I was on my period. There was a realistic option to help preserve what little dignity I had left. People just don't get it, even family.

I also went to MDA clinics about every six months where I would have an appointment with a doctor who specialized in Muscular Dystrophy. These clinics were to basically address any problems I was having related to my disability. Dr. Solis would write me prescriptions for equipment I needed, such as a wheelchair or bath bench (a prescription was necessary for insurance purposes). They would also monitor my health in several ways. They would measure the contractions in my knees, test my arm strength by having me push and pull, and test my lung capacity. I always hated the lung capacity test. I would breath into a tube that would push a lever up and they would read how high I could push the lever. Being familiar with sickness and death through people I had met at MDA camp, the MDA telethon, and clinics at The Institute for Rehabilitation and Research (TIRR), I was always especially paranoid about dying. I knew it would be a horrible sign and a seal on my fate if my lung capacity was decreasing, and blowing into that little blue, plastic tube created a disproportionate amount of stress. The results were always about the same, but that didn't mean I still didn't worry about it every time.

Dr. Solis naturally offered a solution to my period saga when we informed her of it. She suggested I have a hysterectomy. I didn't like the sound of that much more than I liked the sound of wearing diapers. Although I would never be strong enough for natural birth, I always thought I could have a cesarean section. There is also a high probability that the pregnancy itself, labor aside, would not be a healthy choice for me, but with the way technology improves so quickly, I didn't want a solution to my period as permanent as a hysterectomy.

Months after having a period, my gynecologist decided to put me on birth control pills. This way, I could skip the placebos every other month, just start the next month's pills, and so have a period only every other month. Even only having a period once every two months was still too much though. It was amazing how fast the time would pass and before I knew it I would be dealing with the nightmare again.

After taking birth control pills for several years, I began to have ocular migraines. The first time was when I was sitting outside one day reading and all of a sudden I was having a hard time seeing the words on the page. It was strange though, just parts of the letters were cut off. I looked up at my dog sitting in the back yard and I could see her body, but not her head. They only lasted about 45 minutes and would often turn into a regular headache. My doctor was worried they were being caused by the birth control pill, and worse yet that the pill would compromise my health in the future if I continued to take them. It was then that a dream came true. I started taking Depo-Provera shots, a birth control method yes, but also an injection taken in the side once every three months that completely stops my period. No more mess.

Unfortunately, that wasn't the end of awkward changes in my life that were caused by becoming a woman. When I first started shaving my legs, my mom helped me. Inevitably there were times when I would want to shave before going somewhere when my mom wasn't home, and so my dad would have to do it. I can't believe my dad had to shave my legs. I never told any of my friends. As I got older, it was even more embarrassing, and finally we figured out that if we put a trash can in the bathtub, upside down, and put my legs up on it, I could reach my legs and shave myself. I also have a hard time shaving my armpits because it is so difficult to raise my arms, but I just muster up enough strength to do it because doing it myself with difficulty is better than having it done for me.

8

The summer after my sixth grade year came sooner than expected and brought with it what we knew would come soon enough, the inevitable back surgeries. Since elementary school I knew that the day would come when I would have to go through two risky back operations, but the threat of being cut into seemed so far in the future that it was as if it wasn't really me the surgeries would be done on. It was so distant that it did not seem like it would really ever happen. It was hard to even get too excited about the fact that I would no longer have to wear a body brace and so would no longer have to shop for clothes while considering how low the neck came down so the shirt would hide the brace. I also knew that it meant I would be able to purchase my first bra. Although I occasionally had such fleeting thoughts, thoughts of the surgeries certainly were not consuming my time despite the constant reminders that they were sure to come.

Every six months, in addition to being fitted for a new body brace, I would have an appointment with Dr. Dickson at TIRR in the Houston medical center. The visits started by waiting in the general waiting room with other patients who had various appointments with all sorts of doctors. Since TIRR is a rehabilitation hospital, many of the people we saw coming in and out of the waiting room were there as inpatients of the hospital. Many of the people had been in serious accidents or had severe deformities. It was difficult for my family to sit and wait for my name to be called; everyone knows horrible things happen sometimes to people, but who wants to sit and have constant reminders paraded in front of you for two hours?

When my name finally was called, it merely began our journey. We would be taken into a room where we would wait once again, this time in privacy. A nurse would come after a few minutes and escort us to the scale so that I could be weighed. The scale was a huge metal platform that was level with the floor so my wheelchair could be rolled on and weighed. My dad would then lift me out of the wheelchair so the wheelchair could be weighed alone and then its weight subtracted from the total weight. We would then take a trip to radiology where we would be asked to wait, yet again. When the x-ray room became vacant we would then enter and have to remove my body brace. I also had to be taken out of my wheelchair and placed on a stool for the x-rays to be taken. A stool was needed because it did not have a back or sides that would interfere with the x-rays of my back. They also wanted me sitting, without my body brace, so they would be able to measure the full degree of curvature my spine had advanced to. It was difficult to sit without my body brace on, and even more so without the seat having any support for my back. It was even more of a joke when they asked me to take a deep breath and hold it when they were taking the x-ray. I knew if I made the slightest move I would fall right over. The whole process was so physically awkward, I felt like a contortionist.

They had to take several pictures, which included views from the front and the side. Finally they would finish and we would get a break for lunch. This time also allowed the x-rays to be developed and to be given to Dr. Dickson so he could take a look at them before we arrived. After lunch, which was usually spent by my family in the hospital cafeteria, we would wait once again for our name to be called. At last we would see the doctor.

Dr. Dickson was an older gentleman whose bald head, sturdy build, and solid, tenacious demeanor naturally willed anyone in his presence to feel immediate respect for him. The respect also came in part by knowing that his hands had been taught under the instruction of the very doctor who developed the back surgery I was to have, Dr. Harrington. Dr. Dickson had also performed over 5,000 back surgeries, installing Harrington rods to support the spines of many needing patients.

After taking a seat around a large conference table, joined by Dr. Dickson, the man who made my braces, Dr. Dickson's nurse, and a few other ambiguous faces, Dr. Dickson would precede to inform us of my progress. He would tell us the degree of curvature my spine had progressed to, and go over the recently taken x-rays. On the last of these routine visits, we also picked a date to have the operations. My back was grown enough, I weighed enough, and my spine could not afford to get any worse, it was time to finalize the plans.

The dates were set. My first operation would be on June 24, 1992, just a short time after I would get home from MDA camp. In this surgery, known as the anterior fusion, he would make a skillful incision down the length of my right side, and deflate my right lung in order to remove a rib. After the rib was removed, the last five disks in my spine would be removed, and the bone from my rib would be used to fuse together the bottom of my spine, making it solid bone. Many screws and hooks would also be attached to my spine where a cable would then be run lengthwise down my spine.

I would have a week to recover from that surgery and then, on June 30, a second surgery, the posterior segmental spine instrumentation and fusion, would be needed to place the two Harrington rods in my back, one on either side of my spine. We were warned of the risks, which ranged from minor things that could go wrong to paralysis and even death.

After setting the dates for operation with Dr. Dickson, my parents then had to notify our insurance company and do the necessary preliminary bureaucratic bullshit to get pre-certification. Then, one week before the surgery, my parents and several close friends of our family donated blood that would be used, if necessary, during my surgeries.

Before we knew it, all the preparation was over with, it was time for the operations, and we were at the hospital. Upon admittance into a room at Methodist hospital in Houston, the nurses set us up with a video explaining what I would feel like after back surgery and how I would need to be turned in bed, and then how I would eventually need to be lifted. The afternoon spent in the hospital the day before my surgery is really mostly a blur.

That night I had to take a shower in the hospital room and my mom was instructed to scrub my back for ten minutes. As uncomfortable as showers were for me, the excessive scrubbing only made it worse, but I knew it would all be coming to an end. The morning came too soon, and before I knew it I was being taken away from my parents. We had been warned that after the first surgery I would have a tube down my throat to help with breathing, since they were going to be deflating one of my lungs, and that I wouldn't be able to speak. I asked my mom before I left her to give me a sign when she came and saw me to tell me if everything was okay, since I wouldn't be able to ask.

The nurses first took me into a room that had many patients on their beds separated by curtains. This is where they began an IV, and when I took medication orally to begin the process of anesthesia. I was then taken to the operating room where it was very cold and they covered me in warmed blankets.

The next thing I remember was being awake in what I found out to be the intensive care unit. A nurse was rubbing the bottom of my foot, asking me if I could feel her. I somehow signaled to her that I could. I felt so weak that I could hardly move. On my left arm was a sort of brace that was on my wrist, perhaps guiding the tubes into my arm. It made my arm so heavy that I couldn't lift it. The tube that was in my mouth was forcing oxygen into my lung, helping me to breath. Each time it simulated what would have been an inhale though, I was experiencing extreme discomfort. It felt as though too much air was going into my lung, and it would burst. Even as drugged up as I was, the discomfort from this breathing tube was preventing me from dosing off. I was still unable to speak, and could barely even move my arms, but I somehow managed to get a nurse's attention and then get across the idea of what the problem was. After just a few minutes she figured out what was going on and whatever she did, the problem stopped. My breathing became much more natural and I was able to go back to sleep. The next time I awoke was when my parents were allowed to come visit me. They could only stay for a few minutes because I was still in intensive care, but seeing them, even for such a short amount of time, was such a comfort. It was also a very upsetting sight for my parents.

After more time had passed, a nurse came over and informed me that they were going to take the breathing tube out. She removed the tape from around my mouth and told me to breath out as she pulled the tube out. I could feel it come from my insides and drag up all the way through my esophagus until it gagged me on its way out of my throat. What a relief it was having that thing gone. Now I was breathing on my own and I could finally speak which meant I could talk to my parents and express to the nurses my needs.

When the nurses felt I was ready, I was allowed to go to a private room, where I would stay for the next week until my second surgery. Problems with the nursing staff began on my journey to my room. A few nurses were pushing my bed into my room when they carelessly ran my bed into the doorjamb. I screamed out in pain, having just had a major back operation, and my parents stood there helpless, not knowing what to do and in awe that they had even witnessed such negligent behavior.

The next week was spent pushing my morphine button every time it would allow me to do so, and watching the stupid game shows that were afforded to me as a result of cable, an amenity I did not grow up with. I had to be turned often because I would get so uncomfortable, but the mere act of turning me was an intricate process that necessitated the nurses. I was lying on a folded up sheet that they would use to rotate me so that my back would remain aligned. Sometimes though, it seemed as if getting the nurses in my room to help would take an act of Congress. The nurses were apathetic and acted as though they were put out when asked to work. There was definitely a serious attitude problem among the workers where I was staying.

The second surgery came and went. Though two pints of the donated blood were needed, I was in good enough shape to go directly back to my private room, avoiding intensive care on the second round. My mom had taken this whole time off work and lived with me in the hospital. She slept night after night for a month on the cot in my room, showered in the bathroom connected to my room, and never left my side. My dad, who stopped in as much as he could, and stayed with us on the weekends, needed to keep working so money would be coming in from somewhere. The problems with the nurses escalated and only made a very stressful, emotionally difficult time, worse.

My progression to be able to sit again was a slow one that started with a box being rested under me and my bed elevated. After I had put some pressure on my back in this way, I could sit up unsupported, but only for a few minutes. I could sit for longer and longer amounts of time, but it took quite awhile for this recovery to take place.

I was at the point where I could sit comfortably for about half an hour when the doctor wanted me to have x-rays taken. My parents wheeled me, in my manual wheelchair, to the opposite side of the hospital where radiology was, and then we had to wait for what seemed like an eternity until they could take the x-rays. There were so many different positions they wanted me in, and a pause had to be taken between each x-ray to be sure it had been taken correctly. By the time they finally finished and we made our way back to our side of the hospital, I desperately needed to get into bed. I needed to have been in bed thirty minutes earlier. On our way back to the room we passed the nurse's station and told them about the delay and that we needed their help right away to get back into bed. We then went back to my room where we waited and waited and waited. I could not take it any longer and then finally my dad decided that he had seen the technique they used to lift me, and he would just get me back into bed. I was worried about my dad lifting me, but my worries were outvoted by my need to get into bed. Several minutes after my dad put me in bed, the nurses finally meandered their way into my room.

At one time I asked my mom if I had done something to upset the nurses and make them mad at me. Even though I was only twelve years old and extremely drugged up, I could still detect their behavior as being inappropriate or askew. Not long after my mom had to reassure me that I had done nothing wrong, Dr. Dickson stopped in to ask my mom how we were doing. My mom's eyes swelled up with tears as she described in detail the indolent behavior of the nurses. He became infuriated and promised to resolve the problem, mentioning that their behavior was the last thing my mom needed to be worrying about. Whatever he did, the nurses soon after began to act as responsible caregivers being paid for a service.

A month passed and at last it was time to send me home. The things that needed to be done to get me out of the hospital were almost as traumatic as the actual surgeries, and probably more painful since I was awake for them. They first had to remove the subclavian IV, the small tube that they had placed going directly into an artery to be used in place of an IV in the wrist or arm. The latter can only stay in place for about a week, and something more long term was needed for my stay at the hospital. The removal of this slender tube from my artery was for the most part painless, and left only a very small scar.

The removal of the second tube was more painful. It entered my body on my right side and ran into my chest cavity to drain any fluid that may have been tempted to settle in my chest, causing complications. This tube reminded me of a garden hose and felt rather like a garden hose being ripped out of me when they pulled it out. That left a scar too. The last tube was a catheter that had been draining my urine for the past month. Its removal was excruciating.

The good news came when Dr. Dickson informed us that I would not need to wear a body brace at all following the surgery. Although the common practice included patients wearing a brace for about six months after surgery (even able bodied people with Scoliosis usually have to wear a body brace after surgery), my bones were so strong (drinking milk my whole life had paid off) that I did not need to wear one at all.

After a month, I left the hospital while laying on the back seat of our mini-van. My mom sat in the back with me while my dad carefully drove the 45-minute venture back to our house in Katy. I spent the majority of the rest of the summer on the couch in our living room. It seemed easier for me to just sleep there at night and lay around there during the day, than to get in and out of bed and on and off the couch. I also would much rather have been in the living room, a part of the activity going on, than separated, alone in my room. My dad's parents came into town to help out since my mom really needed to get back to work. It was a lifesaver having my grandparents around.

Many family jokes were made about my surgeries. First of all we could not figure out how the doctors removed my rib. Did they just crack it off like when you break a wishbone? And what exactly was the process used to pulverize the bone so that it could be used to fuse my spine? We also, for some odd reason, came up with names for my scars. Since they were incisions we called the one that ran down the length of my back my "decision," and the one on my side my "indecision."

I went back to school in the fall, this time starting seventh grade. For the first time I was at school without a body brace. It was wonderful. I felt like a new woman. That Thanksgiving, my parents and I took a trip to Wisconsin to spend the holiday with my mother's dad. Like every other trip we had ever taken, transportation once again presented a challenge. My parents did not have enough time off of work to realistically drive all the way to Wisconsin; it would have taken too long. Instead, we decided to fly, but we needed to rent a van when we got there. There are very few vans with lifts that are available to rent, you have to reserve them far in advance, and they are very expensive.

My parents decided to just rent a minivan that would be similar to the one we had at home, and they could lift my manual wheelchair into the back. We had decided to leave my electric wheelchair at home because it would be so difficult to transport and we would only be at my grandfather's house the whole time anyway, practically a cabin in the middle of a Wisconsin forest. Although it was somewhat frustrating not be able to freely move about in his house, there wasn't really anywhere to go anyway.

Not long after we got home from Wisconsin I got very sick. I woke up in the middle of the night sweating, with chills, and I knew I was running a fever. The next day, Saturday, I ran a fever of about 102 degrees all day. Sunday, I continued to run a fever, but began to have a difficult time breathing when I was lying down. My breath was very shallow. My parents took me to the emergency room since the doctor's office was closed for the weekend. At the hospital, they proceeded to take many chest x-rays, suspecting pneumonia. After several hours spent filling out paper work, getting x-rays taken, and waiting for a conclusion, I was sent home. They didn't find any problems.

Monday morning, my pediatrician called. My x-rays had been routinely sent to his office over the weekend since he was my primary care physician. He had looked over the x-rays and discovered a crucial mistake the emergency room radiologist had made. Dr. Wexler, my pediatrician, saw I had pneumonia. He figured it must have been missed because my chest x-rays were so hard to read due to all of the hardware in my back from my surgeries. He called my father, who was at home with me, and we had to call my mom at work and tell her that I had pneumonia. Once again, I was being admitted into a hospital.

I spent the next ten days in the hospital, my mom once again staying by my side, sleeping on a cot, and once again not knowing if I would recover. One night my fever reached 105 degrees and not only were the nurses about to give me an ice bath, my parents didn't know if the high fever was going to affect my brain at all. The ice bath was not needed though, the fever finally broke on its own.

A teacher brought over an envelope filled with cards that many of my classmates had made wishing me to get well and to have a happy holiday. I was very disappointed to have missed the last few days of school before Christmas break because there were a lot of fun things planned that week, including a field trip to the theater district to see Charles Dickens' A Christmas Carol.

On Christmas Eve, I was released from the hospital. We didn't even have a Christmas tree yet. I spent the next few weeks still very ill, despite being able to go home from the hospital. I was on a lot of medication, including a breathing treatment that I had to do for about thirty minutes, three times a day. The whole winter break was filled with these breathing treatments and feeling under the weather. I had to cough all the time but did not have enough strength to cough on my own, so every few minutes one of my parent's would push in on my abdomen, giving me enough strength to work the pneumonia out of my lung.

On the day school started again, in January, I had to go back to the hospital to take a final x-ray to be sure all the pneumonia was gone and my lung was clear. The x-ray came back clear, and my dad dropped me off at school in the later morning hours. I went to my English class, and knocked on the door since I couldn't open it myself. One of the students opened the door and called out "Stacy's back!" All of my classmates starting clapping.

9

I had a friend named Kenzie that I had met through MDA camp. She was a year younger than I was and although I had known who she was at camp since I was seven years old, we had become much closer over the past few years. Kenzie had the same form of Muscular Dystrophy as I do, but she was more severely affected. Unlike when I was born, the doctors knew there was a problem as soon as Kenzie was born and they told her parents that they didn't expect her to live past five years old. We would joke sometimes about how she had fooled them, being that she was ten, and then eleven years old. Kenzie and I talked on the phone all the time during the summers, for hours and hours, when we were both bored. She also came over to my house after I got home from having my back surgeries and visited with me for an afternoon. She too was waiting to have the back operations but was so small that they couldn't do it yet. She probably weighed thirty, maybe forty pounds. When I told her that I had gotten to leave the hospital without a body brace, she immediately became inspired to drink milk everyday in hopes that she too would not have to wear a body brace after her surgeries...Kenzie also had been wearing a body brace for years.

Kenzie, being a year younger than me, always used to ask me about the things in my life; a sort of way to find out how it was going to be. The summer I had my back surgeries was the summer before she started junior high, and she wanted to know all about having a locker and all of the other things that went along with junior high school.

I was about to enter seventh grade and, like all of the other girls I knew my age, I had been wearing makeup for about a year. I also had my ears pierced and did all of the other things little girls in junior high want to do to show that they are growing up and becoming independent women. Kenzie's parents wouldn't let her wear makeup or do any of those things though, and she didn't understand. I understood though. Kenzie was the size of a toddler, she had big blue eyes and blond hair. She was an adorable little kid, but her parent's definitely saw her as a fragile child, not as a soon to be teenager who was feeling like any other teenager despite her childlike appearance.

When I started my period, Kenzie was in awe. It was certainly a big deal those few years for all the girls to find out who had started their period and who hadn't, the former seeming so grown up and womanly. Kenzie thought she should start hers in the next year or so, since she was about a year younger than me. I never told her, but I knew she would probably not be starting her period any time soon. I had heard about 18 year olds, though rare, who hadn't started their periods because they were very skinny or athletic. Kenzie was so little, she was no where near going through puberty, she was like a porcelain doll.

The summer after her sixth grade year, she had a big summer planned. She lived primarily with her father and stepmother, and was going to be taking a vacation with them as soon as she got back from taking a vacation with her mother. She had been gone with her mother when she came back into town for just a few days before she was to leave again. Kenzie called me in between her trips, but we didn't talk for very long. She basically told me she would be leaving with her dad soon but that she would call me when they got back.

I was a spoiled only child and was given not only a phone, but my own phone line for my birthday in sixth grade. I think my parents got sick of all the phone calls always being for me! One morning on a weekend soon before school was to start, my phone rang. I went into my bedroom and answered the phone and a lady who referred to me by my name asked to speak with my dad. I went into the kitchen and told my dad that someone on the phone wanted to speak with him. As I sat in the kitchen with my mom, waiting for my dad to come back into the room, I knew that Kenzie had died.

Kenzie, at the age of twelve, had died in her sleep while she was on vacation with her dad and stepmom. Their family had driven in their van to their destination and so had to drive home with Kenzie's empty wheelchair in the van. I was one of the first people Kenzie's mom called when she began to spread the news because my phone number was on their speed dial. My dad got off the phone and told us what I already knew. We all cried.

Kenzie's wake was the first one I had ever been to. There were many people standing all around and her small, pink coffin was in the back of the room. After talking with many of the familiar faces, my parents asked me if I still wanted to go see her. We had discussed how I felt about it at home, before we left, and I had told them I wanted to see her. So when they asked again, I agreed, unsure.

I will never forget what I saw. I was expecting what I had seen on TV and in movies, but naturally it was nothing at all like that. She was a real, three-dimensional person, one who I had known for a long time, who I recognized, and who was so close that I could have touched her. Only, she wasn't there, it was like she was sleeping, but of course wouldn't wake. I could have stared at her for hours.

Her parents had placed her Cabbage Patch Doll in the coffin with her; the same doll Kenzie had been embarrassed that her parents had sent to camp with her just a few months earlier. Death is very bizarre. I cried a lot that day, and I decided not to go to the funeral. I didn't really want to go, and I figured I shouldn't miss school and that could be my excuse.

Kenzie certainly did not leave my thoughts when she was physically gone. I still think about her often. For many years, I would dream about her once and awhile. The November after she died, my family and I went to Chicago to spend Thanksgiving with my Uncle George, my mom's younger brother. We were in Chicago for my birthday too. The night of my birthday I had a dream that we had gotten home at the end of our trip, and I was checking my answering machine. One of the messages was from Kenzie, and her voice was so real in my dream. All she said on the message was that she wanted to wish me a happy birthday.

74

I've always wondered if that dream was really Kenzie wishing me a happy birthday. As I write this, I no longer remember the sound of her voice, and although I haven't dreamt of her in years, I think of her often.

My parents and I visited my uncle George in Chicago about every year. He lived in a loft downtown, in walking distance from fabulous restaurants, and right across the street from a chocolate factory so the tempting aroma would creep into his home. The building had installed a wheelchair lift to get up the first few steps at the front of the building, and an elevator brought us up to his loft. For the most part it was accessible, although I was unable to fit my wheelchair into his bathroom. My parents' backs were always sore at the end of the trips from the difficult lifts that were involved when showering and using the restroom at his place.

After living downtown for several years, my uncle purchased a new home near Wrigley's Field. His move put an end to my making as many trips to Chicago, since his new home was three stories and had steps throughout the interior. We were still able to see him often though since he usually made a trip to see us every year.

Having family visit is always amusing because they never fully know the routines and accommodations my family and I have to make, until they stay with us. Although my bathroom is also the guest bathroom, relatives either have to use my parents' shower or get creative since my bath bench occupies most of the space in the bathtub. One day when my uncle was visiting, he was searching in our medicine drawer for a pain killer. We were all sitting in the living room when he asked us if there was a reason all of the tops to the medicine bottles were off. We were all laughing because he thought it was so strange, and we had to tell him that I am not strong enough to get the tops off, so we just leave them all open.

My friends also experience some of the challenges I face when they go out with me. In junior high, I had a group of friends who would go to the movie theater almost every weekend. Usually I would take my manual wheelchair and I would have to be pushed around, which was very frustrating because I had no independence while my friends were running around. Sometimes the boy I had a crush on would push me around though, and then I didn't mind so much, naturally.

On one particular occasion, there were only about four of us who were going. We bought our tickets, and upon entering the theater where the movie we were to see was showing, we realized that all of the places designated for wheelchairs, which totaled two, were taken. We found a place in the theater where there were enough seats for my friends, and we parked my manual wheelchair in the aisle, next to the seat, leaving plenty of room for people to pass.

While we were waiting for the movie to start, an employee of the movie theater walked up and told me that I could not sit there. I told him that all of the wheelchair seats were being used, and he responded that it didn't matter, my sitting in the aisle was a fire hazard. I asked him what I was supposed to do, the movie theater was nowhere near full, and I had already bought my ticket; I should not have to leave. He then told me that I would have to sit in a regular seat, and he offered to pick me up. There was no way I was going to allow some stranger to lift me, and instead my friend, Audrey, picked me up and put me in a seat. The employee then took my wheelchair to the very back of the movie theater, where it would not be a fire hazard.

Basically, not only did I have to be lifted in front of a theater of staring people, a degrading experience, but I was left, immobile, with my wheelchair no where near me. If there had been a fire, would that have been a wise choice? A potential fire hazard?

During my eighth grade year, my parents found a place to move to. A new neighborhood was being built, and my parents especially liked one of the floor plans that was being offered. My mom, who had gotten a degree from the Art Institute of Houston and did computer aided drafting and design (CADD) at work, was able to take the floor plans, draw them up on the computer, and make a few necessary changes to make the house accessible. My bathroom door was completely moved, squaring off my bathroom, giving me the optimum space to move my wheelchair around. A few halls were widened, as were all of the doors, and the closet rods were lowered in my bedroom.

The builder, who was mass producing these homes, and could have in no way been hurting financially, charged us extra for all of the changes we made. These changes, which were being made to make the house livable for me, not as upgrades, cost us money. It seems like everything is more expensive when you have a disability.

During the few months that it took to be built, my parents and I would drive over to it every few days and watch the progress. It is a good thing we were keeping an eye on it too because all of the changes that we had paid extra for, were done incorrectly. One night we came over and my bathroom counter was much too low. They had to rip it out and start over. Another evening, we noticed that the closet rods and shelf in my closet were at the normal height. Again, they had to fix it. Then, they had my bathroom door swinging in. Not a good idea when there is going to be a wheelchair inside, blocking the door from closing. One thing after another, but they finally got it right, and we moved in.

Every summer I had to wake up early, about the same time I did when I was going to school, because my parents had to go to work, and I had to get up before they left unless I wanted to be trapped in bed all day. Not that staying in bed all day would have even been an option...my mom would never have allowed that because it would not be safe. Although I would have gone crazy in bed for so long, I hated getting up so early in the summers; I was one of those kids who could easily sleep until noon, and I always thought it was so unfair. For the first 4 or 5 hours I would have been awake, I could not even call my friends because they were all still sleeping. So I would take my pillow, put it on the counter, and sleep with my head resting on the counter for hours every morning. This is also how I had to take naps if I was tired when I got home from school during the school year. It was no way to sleep though, not when I had a bed in the next room and just couldn't get in it. Not to mention, sleeping that way always made my neck sore.

The summer and winter breaks were never easy on my dad either. Although he was, and still is, in sales, and had a flexible schedule, he had to come home every day at lunch so I could use the restroom. For many years he was selling chemicals and cleaning supplies to the hospitality industry and his territory was in downtown Houston, a 45 minute to an hour drive from Katy. This meant that when he had to come home for lunch everyday during the summer, he would have to block out time not only to assist me at the house, but travel time to and from downtown. During this huge block of time in the middle of the day, he was unable to set meetings with potential clients or his current accounts. Not to mention that he was driving back and forth from Houston to Katy two times a day.

One summer, my parents hired someone to come in at the time they had to leave for work, hang out while I slept in the morning, get me out of bed when I woke up, help me use the restroom and get some lunch, and then leave. It was a wonderful solution that allowed me to sleep late everyday, like everyone else got to do in the summer, and which allowed my dad to work all day uninterrupted.

Sheila, who we had hired to help out, was diabetic and had to give herself an insulin shot every morning. One morning, I woke up and called for her, but she didn't come. I called again, over and over again, but nothing. I started to panic, not knowing what was wrong, and why she wasn't coming. Then I started to have horrible thoughts that she had not gotten all of the air out of the needle before giving herself the shot, and she had died in my living room. I thought that I would have to lie there until six o'clock that night, when my parents would get home. I continued to scream for her though, and finally she came in. Sheila had just fallen asleep on the couch in the living room.

10

My first day of high school was horrible. I was in tears at the end of the day with thoughts that I would have to return the next day, and every other day for the next four years. It was awkward not knowing people in all of my classes, and trying to find people to help me with my books. As I have aged, I have become much more comfortable with asking strangers for help, but when I was a fifteen year old freshman, I avoided situations where I had to ask for help. Not to mention that the bathroom situation was a nightmare, because there wasn't anyone permanent lined up to help me. Unsure of what to do and who to ask, Mrs. Hunsucker, who had gotten a job at the high school, helped me but told me she would not be able to do so everyday. After all, she wasn't the nurse anymore, and was teaching classes. Helping me with the restroom was not part of her job description or responsibilities. The lunchroom situation was even worse, probably the most traumatic.

The first day of school every year is always a little stressful for most kids because you never know who will be in your lunch, and if you'll have any friends to sit with. This was accentuated for me because I often needed help carrying my food and opening containers. My freshman year, Lauren wasn't in my lunch, and neither were any of my other friends. I didn't know very many people yet, being that it was the first day, and I ended up sitting with a few acquaintances I had from junior high. They turned out to be rather bitchy though and caused me to go home after the first day, hating high school. I asked one of the girls to open my milk for me and she did so, with an attitude, and asked why I couldn't open my own milk. Things got better though, and I found nice girls to sit with at lunch.

Not long after I started high school, I got a new electric wheelchair. I had outgrown my old one, and it was time for something new. Technology had advanced since the last time I had been fitted for a wheelchair, and my new wheelchair was to have hydraulics that supported a layback mechanism. It had a headrest, and with the touch of a lever, my entire seat would tilt back, keeping me in a seated position, gradually lowering my head and raising my feet until I had a clear view of the ceiling.

Although I had become an expert driving my old electric wheelchair, the new one was slightly different, and threw all of my movement off. I had to learn all over again, and I was once again destroying the drywall, this time in our new home.

The first day I had the new wheelchair, I could not even go to school. I was a mess, and I knew I would run everyone over. I needed a day to practice where I couldn't kill anyone. When my dad left for work, I went and got a book that I was reading for school, and thought I'd make use of my new layback mechanism. I decided to just lean back a little to comfortably read. I pulled on the lever, and it started making a horrible noise. It wasn't reclining, but the motor was running, and it wouldn't stop. I was afraid to drive my wheelchair and I didn't know what was going on. I had the cordless phone on my lap, and I frantically called my mom at work. I was afraid that at any moment, it was going to catch on fire, or start reclining leaving me practically upside down. When reclined to its furthest point, my torso is parallel with the ground, and my legs are above my body. If I were to get stuck like that, then what would I be able to do? I was panicking and my mom told me later that she knew it was very important that she remain calm when she was talking to me, even though she felt anything but calm.

My mom was far away at work, and I needed a quick fix. For some reason, she had the neighborhood directory with her at work, and after calling everyone she knew and no one was home, she began to call strangers. She finally got in touch with a woman that we did not know who lived at the end of our street. She explained the bizarre situation I was in, and not knowing what she would be able to do for me, my mother asked if she would go down to our house. During that time I had also called my dad on his cell phone. I figured he would have been long gone by then, but he had been running errands near our house before he was going to his office, and so he was still close to home. My dad and the neighbor arrived at about the same time.

My dad messed around with the cord until he got the motor to stop running. Apparently, I had pulled on the cord so hard that it had pulled out of the box, under my wheelchair, and had shorted out. We permanently fixed the problem by taping the cord to my wheelchair so that I would not be able to pull on it from the point where it connected to the motor, so that would not happen again.

I started going to Student Council meetings during my freshman year. The meetings were before school and so my parents would bring me to the meetings before school started, in my manual wheelchair, and Lauren would push me to the meeting. Then, my school bus would come to my house at the regular time and pick up my empty electric wheelchair. After the meeting, Lauren would push me outside to the school bus and my bus driver would pick me up and put me in my electric wheelchair, right outside, for anyone to see my butt in the air. I hated doing that but it was the only option if I wanted to be involved with Student Council.

After years of not being able to transport my electric wheelchair, my parents finally purchased a used Eurovan, and had a lift installed in it. That was an amazing purchase. My mom and I could go shopping with me in my electric wheelchair and we could look at different things in the stores since she didn't have to push me anymore. One of my parents could also drop me and a friend off at the movies, or the mall, and I could have my electric wheelchair. Having my electric wheelchair with me everywhere, for the first time, made me realize to the full extent what I had been missing for so long.

During one of the first times that I had this new freedom, my mom dropped my friend Stacey and I off at the mall. We had been shopping for a while, and were in Walgreens, looking at makeup, when a strange man approached us. We immediately felt uncomfortable, but it only got worse when he knelt down and took my hand. We didn't know what to do, and he started praying with me, telling me that in my next life I would walk and that this life was full of suffering, but soon it would end. He went on and on and I just wanted him to leave me alone. He told me all about his wife and how she too had physical problems when she was here, but now she was in a better place. He must have been praying for me for 20 minutes when he finally left. I would later discover that such encounters are not uncommon, and I have learned to get used to them.

With the new van with a lift, my parents could take me to school early in my electric wheelchair and I could go to meetings like everyone else. My parents wanted a lot for me, including my ability to become involved in extracurricular activities, even though that meant they had to wake me up at 5:00 every Thursday to get me ready (over an hour earlier than they would normally have had to get up), and then drive me to school. I couldn't just catch a ride with my friends, or even take turns driving...my parents took me every week. As the years went by and I became more and more involved, it got to the point where they were bringing me to school several times a week.

❧

I became very involved with Student Council and a few times that year I went to District Meetings. These field trips allowed Student Councils from high schools all over Houston to meet, have activities, and come up with ideas together. The meetings were a lot of fun, and a great way to become more involved. They were held at various locations, but they were always in buildings with stadium seating to make room for the massive amount of students. Several times, the group from my high school would start to climb the steps to sit up high in the seats, and I would have to ask them to come back down so I could sit with my high school, at the bottom. I was always a little anxious when we were looking for a place to sit for that very reason, I guess because I thought if they really didn't want to sit at the bottom, then they wouldn't, and I would have to sit alone.

Even though I know how long I can go without using the restroom and am as predictable as the ticking of a clock, out of necessity, the school made a special education teacher go with me on fieldtrips. I knew I would never use the restroom on the trip because I would always go just before we left, and I knew there probably weren't going to be accessible restrooms where we were going anyway. So often even the "accessible" restrooms do not even have enough room for my wheelchair and an attendant, especially when the attendant has to transfer me to the toilet. A lot of times it is just easier to avoid having to use public restrooms. Even though I explained this, someone still had to come along, and I was so frustrated that they wouldn't listen to me. I didn't need any special help, and I didn't understand why it would kill them to just let me go like all of the other students, without someone holding my hand. Besides, I knew if I was ever in an emergency, several of my friends who would be on the trip had helped me use the restroom at my house before, and they could just help out. Oh, but we can't forget the ever present fear of liability. During four years of involvement and multiple field trips each year, I never did utilize the "help" that was sent with me.

As the years went on, I became more and more involved with Student Council. My junior year, I ran for president, and I won. As president, I needed to participate in a summer leadership workshop that was to be held in San Antonio. A friend of mine who had also been elected an officer for the following year, agreed to help me for the week in San Antonio.

I had a great time that week, and I learned a lot, but I also felt out of place a lot of the time. Many of the activities were held in this large ballroom, and all of the students sat on the floor. Sometimes it was hard for me to feel like I was a part of the games since I was four feet higher than everyone and could hardly even hear what was going on.

Some of the activities also required everyone to jumble around and find a partner who they had not yet worked with. I couldn't exactly maneuver in the crowd, and sometimes I had a hard time finding a free partner. The most stressful event for me that week though, was the skit. Every group had to come up with a skit, and you had all week to work on it. At the end of the week, all of the skits would be performed in front of the whole group, which had two hundred or more students.

There was a free standing stage where the event was to take place, and the people in charge informed me there was no way to get me on the stage. Already I knew that I was going to feel out of place, down on the floor, in front of the stage. I did manage to get my group to incorporate the area in front of the stage into the skit though, so that I would not stand out, alone. Part of my fear was the typical insecurity that comes with being that age, but I also had concerns relating to being the isolated "girl in the wheelchair."

The night came, and it was our turn. Everything was going great, as planned, and I went forward for my part. I did my thing, and then it was time for me to move over to the side, so that our skit could conclude. I pushed my joystick to drive, and nothing happened. I tried again, and still nothing. The skit was continuing, so there I was in the front middle of the stage, not a part of the skit anymore, just sitting there.

The screen on my joystick was reading right motor, and I knew I must have knocked the right lever on the side of the stage, disconnecting my right motor, which would normally be done to push my wheelchair manually. I waved at a girl from my high school who was in the front row, asking her to come over, but at first I couldn't even get her to come up to the stage because she was too embarrassed. I could feel my blood pressure rising. She was too embarrassed to walk the 4 feet to the stage! I was embarrassed that I was stuck at the front of the auditorium in front of all these people and our skit was about to be over!! Finally she came over and I explained to her what I needed her to do. All of this took place in front of hundreds of students. She fixed the problem and finally I got out of the way, just before our skit ended.

Before I knew it, my friends were all getting their driver's licenses. For most people that is a very exciting age when freedom as they have never known it is right around the corner. For me, it was a very difficult time. Not only was a driver's license nowhere in my immediate future, I was not a part of the freedom my friends were coming to know. While they were getting their first cars and going out for the first time completely unsupervised, I was still being chaperoned by my parents. Understandably, my parents were not about to let my friends who had only been driving for a few months take me out in our van with a lift. Unfortunately, this meant if some of my friends were going out, I was not included, not unless my parents took us. My friends would sometimes innocently talk about a concert they had gone to, or a trip to the mall, or a trip to Galveston where they went to the beach, and I would always be sad that I was missing out on the fun.

Finally, over time, my parents began to trust a few choice friends to drive me around, and over even more time this expanded to just about anyone I wanted to drive me. It was an awesome feeling to be able to drive off with my friends, no parents attached. It was a lot like having a manual wheelchair I suppose. I still needed someone to help me get around, but it didn't have to be a parent. What I really wanted though was the electric wheelchair of cars, my own van modified for me to drive. How many times did I need something or need to go somewhere and my parents didn't feel like taking me and I could have used my own, completely independent, transportation?

I really hated riding the school bus in high school too. If I had my own van I could drive myself. All of my friends either had cars or had friends that they could catch a ride with. I am not sure how it is in other places, but in Katy, when you turned 16, you got a car. Even if it was old and used, it didn't matter. The important, and the "cool" thing was that you were driving yourself around. My van with a lift, the only way for me to get around, was also the van my mom used to get to work. We could not afford to have three car payments, especially since the van note was pretty hefty with the price of the lift tacked on. Both of my parents worked too, so it wasn't like they could take me to and from school. Although they often dropped me off at school, especially my senior year when I was Student Council president and often had meetings in the morning before school, they were working when I got out in the afternoons and so I had to take the bus home. Public transportation options, such as a bus or subway, didn't even exist in Katy. You had to be closer in the city for that to become a reality.

There were certain times when not having a mode of transportation was even more inconvenient and left me feeling even more stranded than I usually did. For instance, there were tests every few years that all students in Texas were required to take, to be sure they were mastering all the skills they were supposed to. If a student did not pass, they would not be permitted to go on to the next grade level. In high school, we took our last TAAS test and were finally done with it. The best part though, was every year when the other underclassmen were taking their last TAAS test, the upperclassmen were not required to come to school until later in the morning, when the testing was over. They didn't want us distracting the test takers. What to do though? The bus only ran its shift early in the morning, and my parents had to go to work long before I had to be at school on those days. Should I just get up at the regular time, take the bus to school, and then sit in the cafeteria, alone, for hours? It wasn't fair. I wanted to be able to sleep in and only have a half-day of school like all of the other upperclassmen. It was a privilege, and I had earned it too.

Sometimes on these days my dad would drive my mom all the way to work and drop her off, work all day himself, leaving her without a car, and then pick her up at the end of the day. When they carpooled in this way, Lauren could drive over to my house in the morning, leave her car at my house, and drive us to school in my van. I loved those days.

It was an awesome feeling to drive to school with my friend and then park, for the day. I remember getting out of the car, locking the doors, and walking to the building feeling so cool. I wanted people to see me. See, I don't always ride the bus! I was just basically experiencing something that was natural for most upperclassmen, but which was so different from my usual bus ride to school. I felt grown up and so independent.

The other time of year that had unusual school hours was finals. Upperclassmen could be except from several of their final examinations pending grades and class attendance. Therefore, for the last three days of each semester, there were few hours when I had to be at school. Once again though, the school bus was running normal hours. There was no way I was going to sit at school for seven hours when I only needed to be there for a two hour final.

One of these days Lauren was taking a final when I was not and so she could not bring me to school. On that day, my dad was also unable to take my mom to work because he had meetings all day, including very early in the morning. I called my friend Miriam and explained to her what was going on. Then we brainstormed. She had a car, but not one that I could get into. So we needed my van. But my family only had two cars, one of which was my van, and both of my parents needed one. It was simple then. Miriam would bring her car over, my dad would drive that to work, Miriam and I could have my van, and my mom could drive her regular car. Simple...until Miriam's car stopped running two blocks from our house when my dad was driving it on his way to his meeting. Of course. So my dad had to run down the street to our house, in his suit. Miriam called her dad and asked him if he knew anything my dad could do to fix it because this had happened once to him. He gave my dad a suggestion and then my dad ran all the way back to the car, discovered that he was unable to fix it, and ran all the way back again. At this point he was already quite late for his meeting. He needed to leave so he took my mom's car. Then, on our relaxing morning off from school, Miriam and I drove my mom over an hour to work, dropped her off, drove all the way back to Katy (traffic wasn't so bad getting home), went out for a quick breakfast, and went to school, arriving only five minutes late. What a friend.

❧

I felt more embarrassed than ever being a senior in high school and still riding the bus, especially because people who didn't know me didn't understand my complicated transportation problem. I really just felt like the biggest nerd. Not only was I riding the bus still, I was riding the bus with all of the students who had mental disabilities. Unfortunately, people make generalizations and form unwarranted opinions, and I knew strangers who saw me thought things that weren't true of me. Although those "strangers" also assumed things about the students with mental disabilities that also weren't true, I have to admit that at age 16, that was not what I was concerned about. Sometimes I just wanted to scream out that I was normal and I didn't belong on that bus. All of the students receiving special education would be taken out to the curved drive where the little buses picked us up and there they would wait for the buses to arrive. I would usually get outside a little later then they would, because I would be in class, but I hated it when I got outside and the buses still weren't there. Then I would think, please, come here before school lets out. Sometimes the buses would be especially late, and the mass of students would start to come out of the building. I wanted to hide. I didn't want people to know.

One day not long before I graduated, we were driving home through a neighborhood, and one of the big buses had just let out a load of students. One of the boys (he must have been a freshman) started waving his arm and screaming things at our bus about how we were all retarded. Of course, even though our windows were down, I was the only one who heard and understood the insults, I was the only one who got pissed off, and I was the only one on the bus who wasn't mentally retarded.

I also hated riding the buses because of the drivers I had over the years. Every year I would get to know the drivers pretty well since I was the only student on the bus they could have a conversation with. Although some years I became friends with the bus drivers, other years were a nightmare. One year in particular I was wary of my driver because she had told me stories about her family that had led me to believe that her and her husband were pretty much drunks, her husband was rather violent, and her son was practically a criminal. Then, one morning I looked in the rear view mirror and saw that her eyes were falling shut! She was dosing off, and I could feel the momentum of the bus changing as her eyelids became heavy and then would snap open. As her eyes would fall shut, the bus would slow down, and then as her eyes opened, she must have realized we were going too slow, because she would then noticeably accelerate. I was so freaked out I didn't even know what to say. I was sitting there second guessing myself, no way was this happening. Then it would happen again. I knew if she completely fell asleep I would scream out, but she seemed to be coming in and out of it. Unfortunately this wasn't just one occurrence either, it happened once or twice a week. I imagine she just wasn't getting enough sleep. I had felt like that before when I was sitting in class, where it was difficult to keep my eyes open, so I could completely understand what was happening, although it was totally unacceptable behind the wheel of a school bus!

Not only that, but I stopped an accident on two occasions that year. Instances where the driver was just completely oblivious to cars about to hit us, and I had to scream out to get her attention. There was an aid on the bus that year because some of the students were so misbehaved, but she sat in the very back of the bus and was unaware of everything I was seeing. I started to freak out that the driver was going to kill me in my last semester of high school and so I contacted Transportation, where the bus drivers worked. You would think they would have been concerned, but apparently they thought it would be a lot easier to just blow me off. They didn't think I was seeing correctly, there was no way she was shutting her eyes. After all, they argued, the aid on the bus hadn't noticed anything. It was so unbelievable, there was no doubt in my mind that she was having a hard time staying awake in the mornings, and they didn't want to hear it. I guess they would rather put all those children at risk who didn't have the capacity to recognize what was going on. The head honcho over at Transportation actually said to me over the phone, "Don't you think maybe you are just tired of riding the bus and so are trying to find a way to get mom and dad to take you?" What a prick. I had never even met that asshole before, and he was accusing me of lying instead of taking a look at the people he was hiring to drive school buses. It's not like my parents taking me to school was even an option anyway, they both worked full time!! I was just trying to stay alive long enough to go to college.

Despite not being able to use it to get to school, having a van with a lift was wonderful. I could go out with my mom, or my friends, and no one had to be strong enough to lift a wheelchair. The only time the lift was inconvenient was in the rain. There was nothing you could do to make the lift operate faster in bad weather, and the only option seemed to be to become drenched.

One evening, Lauren, Miriam, and I had been out seeing a movie, and on the way home decided we wanted icecream. It was pouring outside though, and as we sat in the parking lot at Marble Slab, I contemplated the best way to get inside while staying as dry as possible.

We decided that Lauren should just go inside and buy everyone's icecream and Miriam could wait out in the car with me, so I didn't have to get soaked. The only problem was I didn't know what size of icecream I wanted because I didn't know how big their bowls were. So we told Lauren to go inside and hold up the bowls, and we would flash our headlights at the winner. Apparently there was a misunderstanding though, because Lauren went in and held all three of them at once. Miriam and I were laughing so hard we couldn't communicate to her what the problem was- how could we tell her which one we wanted when she was showing all of them to us at the same time! Finally Lauren figured it out and held up each container separately and we flashed our headlights at the one we wanted. The guy who was working behind the counter thought we were crazy. It worked though...eventually.

Summer always came unexpectedly, and the weeks spent at MDA camp flew by. Before I knew it, I was packing my bags once again. I had had many attendants over the years, they would usually come for a few years and then stop because of college or a job. Beth had been my attendant for a few years, and she and I were good friends, but she was unable to come one summer, and I asked my friend Stacey if she would go as my attendant. She had been hearing my stories about camp since we had been in elementary school, and she was glad to go.

We spent a few days doing the normal camp activities, horse back riding, swimming, sports and games, arts and crafts, and then one morning we got word that one of the campers had been sent to the hospital in the middle of the night. His name was Trey, and he had Duchenne Muscular Dystrophy, a progressive, fatal disease only found in males. Although the boys are born healthy and learn to walk, eventually running around with all of the other children, a noticeable difference occurs usually before they even enter kindergarten. The symptoms can include unusually high frequencies of tripping and loss of balance, noticeably large, swollen calf muscles, and a tendency to walk using the tips of their toes. The muscles deteriorate, leaving the child requiring the use of a manual wheelchair by elementary school. As their arms begin to be as weak as their legs, an electric wheelchair is then needed because they can no longer push themselves. Although the disease manifests differently in many children, the outcome is loss of strength throughout their body, usually drastic weight (muscle) loss, and sometimes even difficulty speaking and eating. The disease attacks every muscle, including the heart. Boys with Duchenne usually do not live to be older than about 21, usually succumbing to heart failure or other complications due to compromised body functions, and we all knew that Trey had to have been almost that old. He had been having pains in his chest when they took him to the hospital, and the next day while his attendant stayed with him, we were all busy making a huge get well card for him and hoping he would be able to come back before camp was over.

That night, Trey died. The next morning, a bunch of us were sitting on the porch of our cabin when a man wearing black with a white collar walked toward us. He asked the boys to go back to their cabin and the girls were all asked to go inside. He then told us that Trey had died the night before. His mom hadn't even made the 4 hour drive from Houston by the time he died and so didn't get to say goodbye. As we sat in our cabin, in a circle, and embraced each other, we sobbed. We all felt the loss that occurred and were in a state of mourning, but for everyone at camp that year that had a form of Muscular Dystrophy, the sadness had an even deeper level. There were many guys who were at camp, who knew they had Duchenne, who knew what that meant, and who knew why Trey had died. What does that feel like? Were some of them in their late teens, early twenties? Even I, who has a very different form the disease, who has the potential to live to be an old woman, had a stark realization when he died. This disease is in our bodies, it attacks in different ways, but the damage it can do is life threatening for most who have it. Though I feel normal and lead a normal life, if I am to get a bad flu that settles in my lungs, and turns into pneumonia, my body, affected by my weakened lung capacity, may not be able to fight the way it was built to. If I can stay healthy, I may live to see grandchildren. But what about all of the other people? What about Kenzie who's frail body never developed fully and was not able to support her enough for her next breath? What about all of the seemingly healthy adults who contract ALS (Lou Gerhrig's disease), another progressive, fatal form of Muscular Dystrophy? When Trey died, we cried all day, and the spirit of camp didn't resume that year. And in every camper who was old enough to understand the connection they had with Trey, a small piece of their spirit left too.

Time passed and my dad's father became ill. He was very old and had had prostate cancer for years, and it seemed that it was finally going to get the best of him. My family and I made the trip to Wisconsin to see him, and once again we had to rent a van without a lift, but this time I brought my electric wheelchair. We stayed with my grandfather most of the time, so my parents didn't have to lift my wheelchair too often. It only took one time though, my mom slipped a disk in her back while lifting my wheelchair just before we went home. She could hardly make it back to Houston, and when we finally did return, she was in bed for weeks.

While it was nice for everyone to be able to say goodbye to my grandfather, it wasn't easy seeing someone who was dying. A hospice worker came in one afternoon and told us what to look for when the time came, when he was dying. I wish I wouldn't have heard the signs that show death is soon to come; it was so eerie. I repeated the words in my head so many times after she left. His limbs will begin to turn purple because his body will be conserving the blood for his organs. My grandfather died a few months later and I stayed in Houston while my parents went to his funeral.

I had been very sick a few times that year, with severe coughs that turned into bronchitis, and had been worried about getting pneumonia again. I was never one to think that I was indestructible, I guess since my disability was evidence that I wasn't. I always knew that death could come at any time and that people with all different forms of Muscular Dystrophy died all the time. Then, after having so much death around me, and thinking about the young people I had known who had died and not been given the chance to do anything more with their lives, I started to have panic attacks. Sometimes I would be lying in bed at night and I would think about my friends who had died, and how someone must have found them that way. What if I died one night? How horrible it would be for my parents to find me. I would visualize my own funeral, my still body laying for eternity in a coffin, the way I remembered Kenzie, and all of my loved ones all around, crying. What would happen to my parents? Would my dad continue to hear me calling for him at night? Would they always wonder what I would have done with my life? Would they ever be happy again with their only child gone forever?

The panic attacks got worse. I was losing sleep over them, and I would even have a hard time breathing when thoughts of death consumed me. I wasn't afraid of dying because it meant I would be dead, but more for the suffering of others it would cause. It was illogical, I was more afraid of the things death would bring about than death itself, and those things I wouldn't even witness because I would be dead. I was inconsolable, and we contacted a therapist who worked with MD patients. I saw her twice. We just talked for awhile and didn't really come to any conclusions, but over time the attacks subsided.

I did go to a support group for people with Muscular Dystrophy, thinking it may be helpful to talk to people about these things. I only went once though. Most of the people in the group were much older than I was, and I felt that the issues I was dealing with at the time were quite different that those issues they were dealing with. The leader of the group had SMA, the same form of Muscular Dystrophy I do, and while it was helpful to see that someone with my disease could live well into adulthood, she had a tube that went into her throat, probably for breathing, and that wasn't something I needed to see at that time in my life. I didn't need to add any worries to what health problems I could have, I had enough ideas as it was.

Now that I have lived for some time with my disability, I feel more sure of what to expect, but when I was younger and I heard about someone needing a feeding tube to eat, or a breathing machine to get air, or an iron lung to breath when they slept at night, I would become uneasy not knowing if those things would be in my future. I still have to remind myself sometimes that no one else's life is guaranteed any more than mine is, and my disability is not a death sentence. Each day just needs to be taken one at a time, and I am grateful for each day I wake up healthy.

Although I was made all too aware of some of these health problems at camp, camp provided many very positive things for me. As I got older, the meaning of camp changed. When I was very young I loved to go swimming and to make things at arts and crafts. As I got older though, the activities didn't exactly excite me. Camp became more about seeing my friends and being able to spend time with them all week.

Camp, in my older years, also provided me with a place where I felt prettier than I usually did. It was a place where the boys saw me for who I was and understood the help I needed. I always thought I would meet my husband at camp.

By the end of the week I would spend at camp, my self-esteem was always higher than it had been all year, and this would even last me for most of the summer. It would usually last until I would go back to school where there were beautiful girls walking around everywhere and no guys were interested in me.

I think that is what it was about camp, there was so much less competition. For the one time out of the year, compared to many of the other girls at camp, I was one of the prettiest and was very popular with the guys. I felt sexy and attractive to people of the opposite sex. This feeling also caught me falling for many male attendants over the years, and getting my heart broken one too many times. Perhaps I felt a little too normal.

11

I first met Seth when I was twelve years old and he was nineteen. Nineteen and sexy. Seth's camper, Ben, and I had become friends and so naturally we would all hang out at camp. The summer I met Seth was the summer I was having my back surgeries and Seth and Ben came and saw me in the hospital. After that we would all always make a point to get together a few times each year, and Seth and I wrote each other letters when he was away at school. I was definitely attracted to Seth, yes... it was a girlish crush.

Over the years, Seth and I became very close and though I was very young, much younger than he, and he had a serious girlfriend (who he is now married to), I came to love him very much. Although our relationship has always been solely platonic, he will always hold a very special place in my heart for being the first man to make me feel beautiful and desirable. He always told me if only I was a little older...and although he was always joking around with me, I had never felt the way he made me feel before, about myself.

As the years passed and more people came and went at camp, Dana, who was sixteen when he first came, became friends with Seth at camp. My attendant during those years was Beth, and we all would spend the week together. We would also hang out a few times during the summer, away from camp.

Dana could have been a model. He was beautiful. Inside and out. It's no great surprise that he took my breath away...and my heart. During the short week when we would spend so many hours together, I would just want to be near him. His mere presence was illuminating to me. One summer, Dana's camper was not able to feed himself, and at every meal, Dana would just casually give his camper a bite, take one for himself, and carry on with the conversation. I was watching him in such a way one night when I realized how much I cared for him. It wasn't just that he was gorgeous, or funny, or charming, but at that moment the kindness and selflessness I saw in him devoured me.

With senior year came prom. I had never had a boyfriend in high school and felt too insecure to ever initiate anything, even with boys who I was interested in. I guess I always felt like no one would ever want to date me because there was always an available girl who had all the qualities I did, plus she could walk. It wasn't like dating would have been enjoyable anyway. What do people do? Go to the movies, where I sit in my wheelchair a whole foot and a half taller than whoever I am with, who is sitting in the movie theater seat? That's real romantic. Rent a movie at my house, and have my parents pick me up and put me on the couch so I can sit next to my date? Or we could just go out to eat, and encounter the likelihood that the restaurant table is so low that I can't pull up close enough to eat, and I drop food all over myself all night. Or, would I have to ask my date to cut my meat like I am a child because I am not strong enough to push down on a knife? No thanks. I suppose if I were to go out with a male friend of mine, that I knew well, that would have been more comfortable, and maybe I could have developed a romantic relationship that way, but high school just wasn't like that. I guess neither is college, where everyone told me boys would begin to see me for who I am, and wouldn't care about the wheelchair anymore. Not so far in my experiences.

Anyway, prom presented a problem. I knew I really wanted to go, I loved getting dressed up, and I didn't want to regret forever that I didn't go to my senior prom. Not only did I want to go to prom, but I wanted to dance. I loved dancing at camp, but I didn't know if I would feel comfortable enough dancing with anyone from school. Then I had an idea. Dana was a cutie, a great dancer, and good company...the perfect date. I loved dancing with Dana at camp, and I knew I would have a great time with him. Not to mention he was better looking than all the high school boys anyway. I called Dana, and after working a few things out with his jealous girlfriend, he agreed to take me.

So I had to find a dress, and I wanted it to be perfect. I have such a small upper body, between my small stature and my lack of muscle tone, it was difficult finding a prom dress. I would have been better suited shopping in the children's department since I weighed about 65 pounds. Not to mention that even after having back surgery that drastically straightened my back, my hip was still noticeably crooked and I felt insecure in any dress that was fitted and that accentuated my crookedness. Lauren and I went to Bridesmart one afternoon, and I saw a beautiful dress. I knew it would be too big, but I figured if it somewhat fit, I could have the rest altered. So Lauren grabbed the dress and we went to the back of the store and asked the saleswoman for a dressing room.

She became very concerned as she looked down at the large step that led up to the dressing rooms. I kept silent, but inside I was thinking how very unacceptable it was to have dressing rooms that I couldn't get to. The lady then went and found a few males who worked there and told them of our dilemma. They then went searching for something to build a makeshift ramp with. They came in with doors and all sorts of wood to try to get me up that step. Meanwhile all of this was taking a long time and Lauren and I, quite irritated, started browsing again. We meandered our way toward the back of the store, where we had not previously been, and before we knew it, we found ourselves going up a ramp to the dressing rooms. When we reached the top of the platform and looked over and saw the men still trying to build a ramp, we called over to the lady. She didn't even realize where we were until we pointed out to her that if you just go around the corner, you can bring a wheelchair to the dressing rooms because there is an incline built into the floor.

Lauren and I were amused. The woman, someone who worked there, had no idea there was even a ramp. Well, at least I was able to try on the dress, because while it was rather big on me, I bought it.

I had the necessary alterations made, found a purse and some shoes, and made a dinner reservation. Then, two weeks before prom, Dana wrote me an email (leave it to a guy not to even call) and said he was terribly sorry but he would not be able to take me to prom. He said that he just realized his Navy formal, with mandatory attendance, was scheduled for that same night. With two weeks notice, I knew I was going to be hard pressed to find a new date. I was very upset about Dana, and everyone I knew had dates already.

I had made plans with my friend Miriam, and we were going to go out to dinner and to prom together, with our dates. I was disappointed that we were not going to be able to rent a limo like everyone else was doing, but I had to go in my van because of the wheelchair lift. Luckily, I had friends like Miriam and her date, Mike, who were willing to miss out on a limo too in order to go with me in my van.

When Dana canceled, it was Miriam who called one of her friends who was a junior at a different high school. Luckily, he agreed to go with me. That is how I ended up, not having even been on a date before, having a blind date for prom. Craig was pretty cute, even if he was a year younger than I was, and he was a very nice guy. I mean, how wonderful for him to have even gone with me. The only downside was, he didn't dance. Since he didn't dance, that meant I didn't dance. I'm not sure if he just felt awkward dancing with me, or awkward dancing in the first place, but I ended up bored, sitting at a table most of the night. Everyone probably thought I wasn't dancing because I couldn't. If only they knew. If only Dana had gone with me.

As my graduation grew nearer, I had to get a counselor at the Texas Rehabilitation Commission. TRC would work with disabled high school seniors to see that they received an education and could then find work so that they too, would become tax payers. My good friend Angela, who I had known through MDA camp since we were very young, and who was a few years older than me, was already in college and was having her education paid for by TRC.

When I first met my TRC counselor, I got a bad impression. We went into her office and she almost immediately told me that she saw me as a normal person who was just sitting down and that she would always treat me like I was normal. Maybe she thought no one had ever treated me normal and her saying that would excite me, but all I could think about was that she would never tell a normal person she was going to treat them normal.

It only got much worse. She told me that the most any student had ever been financially helped for tuition was five hundred dollars a semester. I personally knew many people who had received much more, and I had to fight to get the same benefits. Everything with Danette was a fight. When she finally agreed to pay for my education, I told her that I would need an attendant paid for also. She tried to convince me to just go to the University of Houston, where everyone in a wheelchair lived on the same floor and a bunch of nurses helped them all, but I had higher hopes for an undergraduate education than U of H, and frankly, that kind of segregation didn't sound appealing to me anyway.

She then said she would pay for someone to come in a few times a day to help me. I told her, again, that I needed a full time attendant because I woke up a few times during the night and needed to be turned. At the time I was in the process of getting a van that I was able to drive with severe modifications, that TRC was paying for, and Danette told my mother she didn't understand how I was strong enough to drive but not to turn myself at night. She then suggested that maybe I just needed a little physical therapy and I would be able to do so. You expect such ignorance to surface from time to time, but not by a professional counselor who works strictly with people who have disabilities.

Then she agreed that they would pay for an attendant, but only thirty hours a week, and only for certain services. She then asked me the types of things I would need help with, so she could approximate the hours. I began to list off some things, showering, dressing, using the restroom, doing the laundry. Laundry?!? Well, she exclaimed, they wouldn't pay for that, I would have to do my own laundry. Right Danette. I can barely even lift a pair of jeans.

By this time I had a feeling that Danette didn't like me very much, or my family, and several comments she made led me to believe this. Then, she told me that in order for them to pay for my schooling, I would have to take a series of tests to determine my abilities and interests, before I left for college. TRC had never forced any of my friends to ever take such tests, including the other person with a disability at my high school who was working with a counselor out of the same TRC office, going to college at the same time as I was. Danette told me the purpose of the tests was to show me what my interests were (as if I didn't know), and to show TRC that I was capable of performing in college, since they would be paying for it.

I didn't want to have to take the tests; I already knew what the days would be like, taking tests for people with mental disabilities all over again, but she refused to just look at my high school performance, the 43 hours of college credit I had placed out of through Advanced Placement tests taken in high school (placing me as a sophomore when I started college), or my SAT and ACT scores.

I had no transportation to get to the place where the tests were to be held, but that didn't matter to Danette. She was all too willing to have TRC pay for a taxi to take me all the way into town and back all week. So there was no way out, she was being a bitch, and I could not reason with her boss either. I took the tests, completely unwillingly, not understanding why I was the only one to ever be forced to do so.

The tests were exactly as I knew they would be. I had already earned college credit for calculus, yet I had to take a math test with questions asking me to add 3 and 4, to show

TRC that I could do math. I had placed out of 6 hours of college English, but I had to take a reading comprehension test to show TRC I could read. One section of the test was critical thinking puzzles and the questions got progressively harder. When I turned in the test, the proctor looked at my last answer and told me I was only the second student to have gotten it right...ever.

I should have never been there. Those days were a complete waste of my time and the state's money. Danette was supposed to go over my test scores with me when they came in but she never called me. I wonder why. Perhaps my scores displayed what I had been trying to tell her all along. After many other touchy situations that occurred even after I was in college, word got to me that Danette was no longer working for TRC and I was assigned a new counselor. I was overjoyed.

12

My senior year of high school, my parents and I decided to plan something really big for graduation. The only trips we had ever taken were to see family, and we wanted to do something new. We talked to my grandmother, my dad's mother, and my aunt and cousin, and we all decided to take a cruise. We also decided to take my best friend, Lauren, with us. We contacted a travel agent, found a cruise line that had an accessible ship, and did the necessary financial planning. For months we talked about and planned our trip, and as the time came closer, our excitement grew. We would be gone for seven nights and would stop at San Juan, St. Thomas, San Maartan, and Nassau.

About a month before our trip, a state of panic set in. The previous summer, my wheelchair had been broken when transporting it home from camp. Apparently, when it was lifted out of the eighteen wheeler, it had been set down to hard or bumped, because a small glass chip, priced at three thousand dollars, had chipped, preventing my chair from running. It had been a nightmare because my parents were out of town, so my friend Stacey and I had to get everything taken care of on our own.

I had never flown with this particular wheelchair and for some reason I had the horrible thought that if something happened to my wheelchair on the way to Florida, where we would be flying to catch our cruise, I would be without my wheelchair, and essentially my legs, for the trip.

This paranoia caused me to call the airlines and talk to them about what would need to be done. I spoke with someone, described my situation, and she gave me all the necessary information. She told me the size of the cargo entry on the plane we would be on, and that I would need to somehow get my wheelchair to be small enough to fit through that space.

After some time went by, I called again, with some further questions, and this time I was given different information. I made sure this person knew what they were talking about, and I went with the numbers they gave me. We were going to have to remove the back of my seat, because it was too tall to fit into the cargo, remove my armrests, because they were also too tall, and remove my joystick. Quite a lot of preparation. They also mentioned something about my batteries not being able to stay connected during the flight, something I had already known about from previous flights with an electric wheelchair.

The day we left was filled with excitement. We arose before daylight to get ready and pack our van. We then went and picked up Lauren from her house. We would be meeting my aunt and cousin in Florida.

After checking in our baggage, and waiting awhile for our plane, I decided that I should use the restroom. The small restrooms on the plane make them nearly impossible for me to use, and so I wanted to go just before we left knowing it would be my last opportunity for a long time. My mom and I went into the public restroom, and the door to the wheelchair accessible stall swung in. If I pulled my wheelchair in, I would have been unable to shut the door. My mom and I then found an employee and asked if she had any suggestions. She told us about a changing room that also had a restroom, so that's where we went. Although we could close and lock the main door, my mom had to pull my pants down in the changing room and then carry me through a narrow door into a very small restroom. I have only one simple question. What architect allowed a wheelchair accessible bathroom stall to be built with the door swinging in? Well, two questions. After years of being like that, why hadn't anyone fixed it?

When our plane arrived, it was time for my dad to pull out his tools and start unscrewing the pieces of my wheelchair. He had brought duct tape to firmly tape down the pieces so that everything would stay together. This was especially useful for my joystick, since, although it was taken off my armrest to clear the height requirement, the wires connecting it from my wheelchair were not disconnected. The joystick was just taped to the seat. My dad did all of this while we sat in the general waiting area where people wait to board the plane. We then told the men who would be carrying my fourteen thousand dollar wheelchair down a steep flight of stairs from the plane down to its cargo to be very careful not to bump the chair on the steps, for fear we would have a repeat of camp.

When we got to Florida we had to wait for all of the other passengers to get off the plane before I could be carried off, as is always the case when I fly. Meanwhile my parents had gone to the front of the plane where my wheelchair would be brought up so my dad could put it back together and we could be on our way.

My mom had been gone for a few minutes when she came back to where I was sitting, and she had a horrible expression on her face. I knew something was wrong right away. When I asked her what was wrong all she replied was that the wheelchair better work when dad put it back together. My wheelchair had been carried up and by the time my parents got to the front of the plane, employees of Continental were holding the various pieces of my wheelchair. All of the tape had been removed.

When my dad plugged everything back in, and tightened the last screws, they brought me from my seat on the plane and put me in my wheelchair. I switched the on button up and a message ran across the screen on my joystick: error. It gave some complicated commands indicating what the problem was, but only a specialist would have known what it meant. I tapped my joystick forward, and nothing happened. My worst nightmare had come true.

My dad switched my wheelchair over to manual and pushed it up the incline to get into the airport. We had just a few short hours before the ship was to depart. A customer service employee of Continental was immediately contacted, as was an employee of the cruise we were to be sailing with. We frantically pulled out the yellow pages of a phone booth and started calling any place we thought may be able to fix my wheelchair or supply me with a substitute. It was Saturday, and no such places were open. We were in the middle of the airport, and there were people hurriedly moving in every direction, but as I sat there I felt like time had stopped. I was numb. My mom and I began to cry hysterically. We had been looking forward to this trip for months, why did this have to happen? I was completely helpless. I needed the joystick to work and there was nothing I could do. The whole week would be ruined without my wheelchair. We had brought my manual wheelchair along to use at some of the ports of call, but that wheelchair was uncomfortable, very low to the ground, and awkward for me. Not where I wanted to spend my vacation sitting. My electric wheelchair was just too heavy and had a drag in the wheels that made it impossible to push around. There just weren't any good options.

We called people we knew in Houston to see if they could somehow get in touch with the people who normally maintenance my wheelchair, thinking maybe they could talk us through a solution. We had no such luck. Time was ticking and we needed to catch our ship. I felt a deep depression sinking in and I was completely void of excitement. I told my mom I wasn't sure if we should go; I would rather experience a cruise when I had a wheelchair that was working. We had to decide what we wanted to do and fast. After speaking with the employee of Continental, we decided to board the ship and he would try to find us salvation in San Juan, our first port of call.

When we got to the ship, there was no one around; it was empty and quiet. We were so late that we had missed all of the excitement; everyone was already on the ship. We gave them our luggage, and I could not seem to stop crying. After a short visit to the deck, we went to our room where we remained for the rest of the afternoon. We continued to try to reach some people in Houston to see if someone could help us. The calls from the ship were nine dollars a minute. We finally contacted Angela and her family, but they were unable to get in touch with anyone who could help.

I didn't explore the ship, or participate in the afternoon activities. Neither did my parents or Lauren. Instead, we all sat in my room, very upset. That night, my dad pushed me to dinner and I could hardly enjoy myself despite the wonderful cuisine. After dinner, I couldn't really do anything, so we just went back to our rooms, and went to bed. The next day was spent sitting motionless outside, near the pool. It would have been impossible to get me in and out of the above ground pool, and so I just sat outside, unable to cool off in the pool, or go participate in any of the other activities.

Finally, the next afternoon, we were to arrive in San Juan. The customer service employee at Continental had contacted someone who worked for the company that manufactured my wheelchair, and he was going to be coming on board to try to fix my wheelchair when we arrived in San Juan. It was about four in the afternoon when we got there, and we had to wait for quite some time before the man was able to get on board. When he got to our room, I explained what had happened. There was obviously a problem with my joystick that needed some reprogramming. He tried many things to fix my chair, and for about an hour, nothing seemed to work. If he was unable to fix it, I had decided that we should just fly home from San Juan.

Finally, he had another idea, and this time it worked. He told me to turn on the power and try to drive my wheelchair. When I did, it took off. Mt heart was racing. I drove my wheelchair down the hall, turned it on and off, and it seemed to be running just fine. What a lifesaver he was. I was so paranoid for the rest of the week that I was going to hit something wrong and cause my wheelchair to stop working, but nothing ever happened. The rest of the trip was spent quite enjoyably, as it should have been.

Upon our return to Florida at the end of the week, the same man who had been working with us when my wheelchair was first broken, an employee of Continental, greeted us once again. He told us that the problem had been in my wheelchair, that when the batteries were disconnected, the memory had been lost, and that was a malfunction on the part of my wheelchair. Despite that, he felt horrible it had happened, and he gave me a three hundred dollar voucher for a plane ticket, and moved my family to first class for the return trip.

When we got back to Houston, my electric wheelchair started up just as it should have. However, when we picked up our luggage, and my manual wheelchair, the frame on my manual wheelchair was bent so badly that the back wheels would not even roll. It had been crushed in cargo. So we had to go to customer service and show them that my wheelchair was broken. What the hell was their problem? We were really in awe at our bad luck and could not believe everything that had happened.

Upon closer examination of the events that had taken place we became very angry. First of all, the malfunction was not in my electric wheelchair. On the way back to Houston, the batteries had been unplugged and it did not cause a loss of memory in the computer of my chair. That was a bogus explanation used to divert from the fact that they had obviously tampered with my wheelchair. The problem had been in the joystick, the very piece they had un-taped and were holding. Wires were disconnected that should never have been touched. Secondly, due to their negligence, my parents, and my best friend and I had missed out on two and a half days of a very expensive vacation. The emotional turmoil we went through in itself, was worth more than they had offered. So they gave me a plane ticket voucher, a limiting "gift" to me being as it is so difficult to travel alone because air travel is completely inaccessible to travelers with disabilities. Who would take apart my valuable wheelchair that I depend so much on if I were traveling alone? Who would carefully put it back together? Who would carry me on and off the plane? And even if there are specific trips where I can arrange these details, shouldn't I be able to independently travel like every other person who is able to purchase a plane ticket? Why on earth can I not ride my wheelchair on to the plane, stay in it throughout the flight, and roll off the plane when we get to our destination? Instead, they take me away from my legs and then break them. It is really infuriating.

Not to mention that Continental gave us first class seats on the way home. The seats were obviously vacant if they had the room to move us into them, and so they were not missing out on any money by doing us the favor. Is a two hour flight in a leather seat rather than a fabric one enough to make up for the mistake they made?

I didn't think so. When we got home, I wrote two lengthy letters to Continental. The first applauded the man who had helped us so much. The second explained the financial and emotional costs they had brought on and asked for compensation. We had saved up enough money for such a trip, and essentially we threw away several thousand dollars while four members of our party were depressed for two and a half days, unable to enjoy our money's worth. I couldn't even get around on the ship. That is in addition to the highly priced phone calls we had to make. Continental never responded to my letter.

13

There was one other student when I was in high school who was in a wheelchair and who was in all mainstream classes. He also had Muscular Dystrophy, I think he may have even had the same type as mine. I can't even say how many times people asked me if Craig and I were going to "hook up," like only wheelchair people can date wheelchair people or something. While people at school may have thought that would have been cute, I knew I would never agree to date someone else in a wheelchair, especially when I got older. There would be too many things that wouldn't work if my boyfriend wasn't able to pick me up and throw me over his shoulder. Well maybe not throw me. Anyway, Craig didn't have to ride the bus as much as I did because his father worked at the school and he could catch a ride a lot of times with him. During my senior year, Craig was the one who brought me a flicker of hope about driving myself. He had been fitted for a van he could drive and they were in the process of getting it. I knew then that I had to get one too.

The modifications for me to be able to drive were going to cost about fifty thousand dollars, but TRC agreed to pay for the modifications. I had to supply the van though, and they would only put their expensive modifications into a new van. I had started receiving social security every month when I turned eighteen and my parents figured with my contribution, they could afford another car payment.

The process of getting a van I could drive was a lengthy one. I had to meet with someone several times who worked for a driver's rehabilitation company. He had a van with all

121

types of modifications in it that he used to find out what each individual would need. This is when I drove for the first time, after taking the test and getting a permit at the age of eighteen. He took me out in his van and it was really quit terrifying. Terrifying, but also incredibly exciting. For many afternoons I would drive his van until he determined what I needed. He then had to give the information to TRC so they could release a purchase order to the company that would build the modifications. Meanwhile, I had purchased a van that already had a lowered floor and a ramp in place.

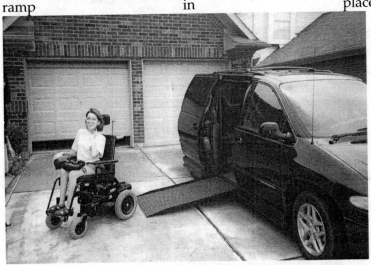

We also had to make some decisions about the van. The main choice to be made was whether or not I wanted to keep the airbag on the driver's side. Although the airbag was in place for safety, I would be sitting closer to the steering wheel than the average person, and I was also shorter and weighed less than the safe norm. I decided to take the airbag out. If it ever deployed, I figured it would probably be for something minor like a rear ending, and I was afraid it would do more damage to me than the accident.

All of this took months. I knew that I would not be getting my van before I graduated from high school, but I was hoping it would be ready by the time I went to college. After months of paperwork, whiplash from my driving practices, and much anticipation, my van was delivered to my house the day I left for college.

What an amazing piece of equipment. There was a small box on my keychain with a button I would push to unlock the doors and then another button which would slide open the side door and lower the ramp down. I had a large screw that had been installed under my wheelchair, and an easy-lock system in my van, so I would just pull in and my chair would lock safely into place. With the push of a button, no keys needed, I would start the ignition. The steering wheel, which I controlled with my left hand, was five inches in diameter and lay horizontal, close to my body for easy use. My right hand controlled a throttle which, when pushed forward would accelerate the van, and when pulled back, would brake. At my fingertips were buttons used to honk the horn, turn on my headlights, turn on my turn signals, turn on my windshield wipers, and buttons with every other function I needed.

When the van was delivered, I took my parents and Lauren for a spin to show off my driving ability, and then I parked it in front of my house where it would have to stay when I went to school. I was in no way ready to drive it to Austin.

For the next couple of months I drove it a few times in Houston, on the weekends, and had several of the usual near misses new driver's experience. The steering wheel had no resistance so that I would be strong enough to drive it, but it made losing control around curvy roads a little too easy. At one point, my mom was sitting in the back seat and I lost control for just a moment, and all she could see from behind was my bobbed hair flying back and forth. I don't know how I didn't kill my whole family.

Another time my dad and I were driving and there were two stop lights on this inclined road, one right after the other. I didn't even see the first one, which happened to be red, and I started to drive right through it. My dad reached over and yanked my throttle back, slamming on the breaks, stopping us in the middle of the intersection. Luckily for us, no one was coming, but we screamed at each other for the

124

next hour. If he hadn't taken over we would have been better off, and I yelled at him because he never would have put his foot on the brake pedal if I had a brake pedal!

One time I was driving with my dad and we were on a curved overpass in Houston when I fell over to the side. My dad had to hold me up, but I told him not to push me all the way up because I was driving 60 miles per hour on this overpass, and if he pushed me up it would throw me off. So I finished the curve and then he pushed me up straight. At that point we realized I didn't have enough upper body strength and in addition to my lap belt and cross belt, I started wearing a lumbar belt that secured my whole upper body to my wheelchair.

After awhile, the person who had been training me to drive brought my van to Austin where I then drove it around more. He also went with me when I finally got my driver's license. I drove my van around Austin for about a month, taking my friends out shopping or to dinner; wherever we were going. I even made the trip to Houston and back again with my dad one weekend. I was hoping to drive my friends back home for Thanksgiving, but I wasn't comfortable making the trip for the first time with them. I wasn't sure if I would get tired driving for that long, but I did fine when I went with my dad.

Three days before my nineteenth birthday, the week before I was going to drive all of us home for Thanksgiving, two of my friends, Gisela and Donna, and I decided to go shopping at Old Navy, a clothing store about ten minutes from the dorm. The parking lot was in sight and just as I was going through the last intersection, I hit the curb, had a blowout, and lost control of the van. It all happened so fast, the jolt from hitting the curb threw my body, but for an instance I didn't think it was a big deal, that I would just recover control of the car. Before I knew it though we were veering to the extreme left, cutting across lanes of traffic,

125

and before I was able to take control of the van, we slammed into a light pole.

We had crossed three lanes of traffic at a green light, skimmed the rear bumper of someone's car, and hit the pole, coming to a dead stop, from about 40 miles per hour. The lumbar belt had kept my upper body firm, but I had forgotten to fasten the lap belt on my wheelchair, and so my lower body slid forward. My back was in a lot of pain and I needed to be pulled up into a straight sitting position. Gisela had seen the smoke from her airbag deploying and was afraid the car would explode so she had jumped out of the car. I called out for Donna who responded and I asked her to pull me up from my under arms. She grabbed me under the arms but she couldn't seem to pull me up and I was in so much pain.

By that time there were people standing all around, and a stranger crawled in to the passenger side. I was unable to release the switch on my wheelchair and I couldn't get my wheelchair to back up. I was trapped. The man leaned under my wheelchair and manually unconnected my chair from the van. Someone then pulled me up.

I later realized that the reason the release switch wasn't working was because the ignition was still on and it was built not to release if the car was on, as a safety device. We also later realized that Donna couldn't pull me up because she had a broken wrist. She hadn't been wearing her seatbelt and she had fallen forward when we crashed, breaking her wrist, busting her lip into two pieces, and bruising her legs. Gisela walked away fine and didn't even have to go to the hospital. I'm very glad I had the airbag on my side removed; I'm afraid what may have happened if it hadn't been.

The ambulance came and I told them that I had rods in my back from surgery and that my back was in a lot of pain.

They lifted me out of my wheelchair and put me onto a stretcher, Donna got into the front of the ambulance, and we left for the hospital. My van was left with the sliding door open, the ramp somewhat down, and my wheelchair in it.

When I got to the hospital I was left alone for a few minutes and I was so terrified. I didn't know what was wrong with me, or if I was going to be okay, and my parents were two hours away. They took a bunch of x-rays of my back and didn't find any broken bones. They were unable to detect if there were any fractures and they weren't sure what was causing me so much pain, but they knew that I was going to be okay. During this whole process, a social worker at the hospital was trying to get in touch with my parents, leaving numerous messages on their cell phones. They also contacted Ashley, my roommate.

My parents had been in the theater district in Houston seeing a performance they had acquired some tickets to through some friends. When they got into their car and saw how many messages were on the phone, they knew something had happened. My mom started listening to all of the messages and had no idea if I was alright, or what exactly had happened. They got in touch with me at the hospital and they said they would be there in a few hours. My parents then went home, made some coffee, packed a bag, and left for Austin at 11:30 at night.

Meanwhile, the hospital was ready to discharge me, but there was a problem. My wheelchair was in my crashed van at a junkyard 45 minutes from the hospital. When I first got my new van, my parents put an ad in the paper to sell our old van with the lift. It's a good thing it hadn't sold because we now still desperately needed it. The social worker at the hospital eventually contacted a taxi driver who had a van with a lift. He was booked until about one in the morning, but he agreed to go get my wheelchair out of my van and then come get me and bring me back to the dorm. We got back to the dorm just a few minutes before I was expecting my parents to get into Austin. Ashley and our friend Nicole met us at the front door and asked if we were okay. Donna replied, "Well, we're going to be okay but Stacy will never walk again." We laughed about that one for months.

Gisela, Donna, and I talked that night about what was going through our minds as we were plummeting toward that pole. We were cracking up as we imagined the dialogues...Gisela looking at that pole thinking, "I don't think I have my seatbelt on, we're gonna hit that pole and I'm gonna go flying," Donna counting the cars we were dodging as we crossed traffic, and my own panic, "I have to stop this car, I have to stop this car."

My parents came and picked me up and then we went and got a motel room for the night. We made the trip back to Houston the next day, on Saturday, and I stayed at home until the next weekend, after Thanksgiving. My back was still very sore. I had sharp pains that went down my spine every time I was lifted or I hit a bump in my wheelchair. I could barely drive over the bumps in the house that separated the carpet from the linoleum. I mostly stayed in bed anyway.

The drive back to Austin was the killer. I was in tears the whole way back, because for two hours, all the way to Austin, every bump the van hit on the road sent shooting pains down my spine. I thought we would never get there. Then I could barely ride the lift to get out of the van when we did get there because it would thrust forward so drastically, jarring my back. The pain was more excruciating then when I had the back surgeries...maybe just because this time there was no morphine.

The next few weeks were ridiculous. I attempted to go to class, but I had to go so slow to not be in pain that it wasn't worth the trip. Ashley's lift hurt even more than my dad's had, probably because she wasn't as strong and so couldn't support my back as much as he did. I called my parents crying, telling them that I might have to come back home, but I didn't know what would happen with school if I left. My friend Melissa transferred me to bed one night and my back didn't hurt as much when she lifted me, so she started to help out whenever she could. We didn't have much time left in the semester, and my back began to slowly heal. I finished up what I needed to and went back home for the winter break.

The decision needed to be made, would I drive again? Was my accident a sign from God that I wasn't meant to drive? He had spared my life and the lives of everyone involved, but would He next time? Or should I get back on the horse? My mom had been terrified during the whole process of my getting a van, never sure if I should have been behind the wheel of a car, and although I was sure she would support whatever decision I made, I knew she didn't want me to drive again. My dad was less convinced, one way or the other, and surely would have allowed me to make a decision on my own. I spoke with my friends and was given support to do what I felt I needed to, but many had advice much like Seth, that most people get into an accident when they are first learning to drive and I should try to not let that scare me into never driving again.

I really did not know what to do. I loved driving, but I also often felt out of control and afraid. I did not have the confidence in my driving ability to convince myself that I wouldn't kill someone. I wasn't concerned about getting on the freeway, or making lane changes, or parallel parking. I was afraid my arm would give out as I was driving on a curved road, or that I would get tired while going 70 miles per hour on the freeway and lose control. I was a good driver; I just wasn't strong enough for driving to be safe. Meanwhile, our insurance company made estimations of the damage at twenty thousand and started repairs. The van was so new that its value was still more than that so they did not total it.

For several months while the repairs were being made, I was still trying to decide what to do. The time was nearing when I would need to decide. Before I knew it, it was February and it was scheduled for me to get refitted for my van, which was near completion. Though I had not made an official decision, not wanting to have the power to make such a crucial decision, things were just happening and I was going to be getting my van back.

I was scheduled to go back to Houston the following weekend to pick up my van when I got a phone call from my parents. The insurance company had gone out to see my van one last time before they released it when they found ten thousand more dollars of damage. The frame of the van had been bent and they felt the integrity of the van had been lost; almost three months after the accident, they totaled it. No decision needed to be made.

Though I suppose I could have started the whole process all over again, the fact that I had considered driving again when my van was finally totaled was a second sign as far as I was concerned. I chose to wait until technology advanced further and resumed being driven around in the Volkswagen, which luckily we still owned since it had not sold.

14

My senior year of high school, I knew I was a shoe in for many universities. I was in the top ten percent of my class at a large high school, I was Student Council president, I did community service, and my ACT and SAT scores were competitive. The problem was, I knew that I could not go to any college I wanted to. I had spent holidays in Chicago, and I knew that living anywhere with that kind of cold weather was not realistic for me. I wasn't willing to go months out of the year not being able to move because my arms were so weighed down by a coat that was heavier then me.

I also knew that I would have to find an attendant to take care of me, wherever I decided to go. I had no idea how to go about doing that. Where do you look? Who do you talk to? How do you know until you are in the situation that the person you do find is going to be trustworthy and responsible? You don't. I guess in a way I allowed my fear to limit my possibilities. I just couldn't imagine going to another state to go to school, somewhere where I knew no one. Who would I turn to if my attendant wasn't doing an adequate job? I had heard horror stories about attendant care, from people showing up late, coming to help only when they felt like it, and sometimes not showing up at all.

And so I decided to find a university in Texas. It saddened me in a way because there were other schools I was very interested in, but my need for security overcame my desire to travel. After visiting a few campuses I only applied to two schools, Rice University and the University of Texas. I was very excited about my Rice application. The campus was beautiful, the school was prestigious, and I would be close to home. I didn't give UT much thought because I was guaranteed admittance being that I was in the top ten percent of my high school class.

I applied early to Rice in hopes of increasing my chances, and waited patiently for a letter of acceptance to come in the mail. Instead I received a letter asking me to reapply for regular admission; I hadn't been accepted but I hadn't been denied either. So again I waited for months. Finally a letter came once again. This time it told me the same news, I hadn't gotten in, but I hadn't been denied either; I had been put on the waiting list. After months of waiting, I knew I needed to secure another plan.

I had been accepted to UT and arranged for housing, but I had one arrangement left to make. I needed to find an attendant. I knew a few people from my high school that were going to UT, and although none of them were close friends, I asked around to see if anyone would be interested. I got little response. I then placed an ad in the Daily Texan, the university newspaper. I also contacted someone in the nursing school, asking her to put up a flyer. I received a few phone calls, but there was always some reason or another that it wouldn't quite work out.

I contacted the housing department on campus and they were of no help. Although they used to assist people in finding attendants, they now found it to be a liability in case things didn't work out with the attendant they selected. What isn't a liability these days? Then I found a student who was interested in helping me but was going to be graduating in December, so I would have had a fix, but only for one semester. An employee of housing tried to tell me that they would not let me move into the dorms unless I had an attendant set up for the whole school year. I then kindly informed them that there was no way they could deny me a whole semester of education, having an attendant lined up and everything, just because I didn't have a plan for the following semester. They wisely agreed.

Before I knew it, it was the middle of the summer and I had not found anyone yet. I signed up for orientation, knowing that if I didn't find someone I would be unable to go to school in Austin. My best friend Lauren went to orientation with me and helped me for the three days, but she was not a permanent answer since she had been accepted to the University of Southern California in Los Angeles. In the back of my mind I thought maybe I would be able to find someone at orientation. I had no such luck.

In fact, not only did I not find anyone to be an attendant, but I had my first eye opener as to how the general public feels about people with disabilities. One of the activities one evening was a speech given to a group of several hundred incoming freshman about all sorts of touchy subjects. To drive her point home about prejudice and discrimination that exists, the speaker insulted everyone in the room. She had comments about women, African American people, Asian people, gays and lesbians, people with disabilities, Jewish people, you name it. It was very powerful. Then she asked people to stand in complete silence if they agreed with a statement she would then make. She then proceeded to make remarks such as, "I am afraid if I am alone in a parking lot with a man," and if people felt that way they would stand. She asked a series of questions that showed the attitudes of the people in the room, but when she asked if anyone felt uncomfortable around people with disabilities, and several people stood up, I realized what a huge gap many people see between themselves and me. It really is very similar to any other prejudiced attitudes that plague this world. There was a time when many white people felt that they were fundamentally different from black people. I suppose some unenlightened people still feel that way.

Some people also feel that way about people with disabilities.

Racial segregation. People, based on the color of their skin, were not a part of the rest of society. It didn't matter what they did, or who they were, they were to use different facilities and were segregated on every level. Not very long ago, I was at an apartment complex, at the information office, and there was a sign right next to the front door and its six steps that led up to it, "Disabled customers may enter at the rear entrance." A few weeks later I had to go to the doctor and upon entering the office, whose door I could not open, I discovered that I could not even see over the counter to sign in. It seems to me there is a less talked about minority that doesn't have equal status in this country.

Time was running short and I was starting to really worry. I had always figured it would just work out, I would find a roommate, but I was becoming less and less sure. One afternoon, I was talking to Seth, telling him the difficult time I was having finding someone and that I was running out of time. He told me that his sister, Ashley, went to UT and that he was pretty sure she wouldn't mind helping me out. I had met Ashley a few times before but didn't really know her very well. I called her that day and after we talked about it, she agreed. What a relief that was.

It is actually very interesting to think about why she agreed. What was different about her than every other person I had approached? She had volunteered at MDA camp and so knew something about what it means to help someone with a disability, but did she really know what she was getting into? What a blessing she was, I was so thankful that such an understanding, giving person had been placed into my life.

I was so relieved that I would be able to go to college, but my relief was not free of worry. Would Ashley be strong enough to pull up my jeans underneath my dead weight? Would she be able to lift me without bruising my ribs from squeezing me so tight? Would she wash my hair properly, scrubbing my sudsy scalp and then rinsing it thoroughly? Would she turn my hip at just the right angle in bed and comfortably position my legs before a night's slumber?

Although Ashley came to my house before we went to school, to be sure she would be strong enough for a basic lift, I wouldn't know the answers to my questions until I would be far away from home.

I now had a roommate, but I thought I better make a trip to Austin and check out the accessibility of the dorms to be sure that they would work out. I contacted the housing department and they set me up with someone to show me a room. We drove in from Houston and first met with someone from housing and Mike, who also used a wheelchair and who worked for the Services for Students with Disabilities office. We met at Jester, one of the dorms, and took a look at the accessible rooms. The bedroom was very small but would have afforded enough space if the beds were to remain bunked. The problem was it is very difficult on a person's back to lift me in and out of a bunked bed because the person has to be bent over while they are holding me to keep both of us from hitting our heads. There would not have been enough space to un-bunk the beds. The community bathroom did not even have a toilet stall big enough to fit my wheelchair. I was beginning to be very glad we made the trip since the very room I was looking at was probably where they would have put me, and it wouldn't have worked.

We then went over to Kinsolving, an all girls dormitory on the other side of campus. It was the only other dorm that had wheelchair accessible rooms. Kinsolving was divided into two sides, one had rooms with their own bathrooms shared by two sets of roommates and were known as suites. The other side only had community bathrooms. The latter was the only side with accessible rooms. The bathroom was much better than the previous one we had seen, and I knew it would work out. The accessible room however, once again, had bunked beds and movable furniture, what they called the ADA rooms and furniture. When asked if there would be enough room to un-bunk the beds in those rooms, housing answered that it was unlikely.

It just so happened that the student who was showing us the rooms in Kinsolving was a student who used a wheelchair and who lived in that building. She showed us her room, which had an accessible sink like the ADA rooms, but had "normal" furniture which included built in beds and desks, not bunk beds. She told us that type of room had worked out much better for her, and I thought that was what I would need too because of the beds.

When I told housing that the most accessible room for me would be one with a roll under sink but built in furniture, they immediately put up a fight. They claimed that those were not ADA rooms, and since I used a wheelchair I had to use an ADA room. I thought that was about the most ridiculous thing I had ever heard. I was telling them what I needed and they were telling me what I had to have. They were assuming that they knew what would be best for me. I explained that I could not use a bunk bed and I saw the other furniture as the only option. After much disagreement, they agreed to let me have one of the rooms with built in furniture, but I had to sign a waiver since I wasn't going to be living in one of the rooms made for me.

Some of the things they were coming up with during this period of disagreement must have been pulled out of thin air. They complained that the reason all this was happening and we didn't see the right room the day we came in from

Houston to look at rooms was because we had shown up so late that the people had left. Whatever. We had been a few minutes late, but everyone was still there and it was only by chance anyway that we had seen a non-ADA room because of the person who was showing us the rooms. Here I was, I hadn't even started school yet and they were making me feel like I was the biggest pain in the ass, just trying to make trouble, when I was only trying to find somewhere to live.

Before long, the time came, and my parents were dropping me off at school for the first time. Our departure was emotional. I was going to miss my parents terribly. I was also going to miss my comfort zone until I developed a new one. I knew that all within the next day, Ashley would be seeing me naked for the first time when I showered; Ashley would be getting me dressed for the first time; Ashley would be putting me in bed for the first time; and Ashley would be helping me use the restroom for the first time. I wasn't too concerned about the restroom part though, more people had helped me use the restroom over the years than I can count on all my fingers and toes.

I also knew that I would have to explain to Ashley, practically a stranger to me at that time, my unusual bowel habits. I would have to tell her that in the mornings I would need to be left on the toilet for ten or fifteen minutes. Unlike other people who can use the restroom whenever they feel the need, if I don't go in the morning, I may need to go later in the day when no one is around to help me. I have had to hold it for hours one too many times, and I would much rather just sit on the toilet for awhile in the morning and clean out my system than have to spend an afternoon with that kind of discomfort.

In addition to all of my worries, I only thought the housing department hated me at that point. I moved into my non-ADA room when school started, and I was very uncomfortable. The sink had a curved in ledge, instead of a flat surface, and it made it practically impossible for me to wash my face because there was nowhere for me to rest my elbows, and I wasn't strong enough to hold up my arms. My arms would continually slip off the edge of the sink. It's amazing the smallest details that can make the biggest differences, things that even I do not know to look for. Also, all of the shelves in the room were out of my reach, so I was unable to access any of my school books, and the bed that slid partially into the wall left little room for my much needed egg crates. Then, to make matters worse, we met some other students who lived on our hallway who also lived in the "ADA rooms", and it turns out, there was a way to arrange the furniture in such a way to un-bunk the beds and still have room to get inside.

Why hadn't housing known this? How was I supposed to have known? After I saw that the beds could be un-bunked, I knew that I would be much more comfortable in a room with that kind of furniture. I would be able to have a sink I could use, shelves I could reach, a bed I could put egg crates on, AND we would not have to deal with trying to lift me in and out of a bunk bed, the very obstacle I was trying to avoid when I had requested a non-ADA room. So I contacted housing and they moved us into a vacant ADA room. I can only imagine their "I told you so" thoughts. Oh well. Although we moved into an ADA room, and separated the beds, there was very little room to move around. I could barely turn my wheelchair around; we were very cramped. We even had them remove two dressers, not that we could afford to have any less storage space. Then, a few weeks later, Ashley and I were talking to a few girls who lived in a three-person room down the hall. They had different furniture than we had ever seen, and it allowed them to stack the pieces so, for instance, a bed could be put on top of a desk and dresser, doubling the free space. Once again, I contacted housing and found out, on my own, what we needed to do to get such furniture. They changed out the furniture, and finally we were comfortable. We had room to breathe. I am so grateful we happened to see that furniture. It's not like we were getting any help from anyone from the housing department, although surely I wasn't the first person in a wheelchair to live in the dorms at UT.

When you have a disability, it is often very necessary for you to be your own advocate, to do your own research and investigation, and then to insist and persevere. I imagine that a lot of people with disabilities probably live in situations that are much more difficult and exhausting than necessary because they are too intimidated and shy to speak up for themselves. Although it does sometimes seem like life is just one battle after another, and sometimes I get tired of fighting, I also understand that this is my life and I am going to do what I can to make it as positive an experience as possible. Sure, with disability comes limitation and obstacles, but I find that the vast majority of the difficulties I encounter are avoidable with the proper modifications and accommodations, meaning that many of my frustrations arise from barriers imposed by society, not Spinal Muscular Atrophy.

For the most part, living in the dormitory worked out pretty well. I certainly had true independence for the first time. Since I lived, and went to school, all within walking distance, I could go where I needed to when I needed to. If I had a review for a test in the evening, I just went, by myself. I didn't have to depend on anyone to get me anywhere; I even had stores at my fingertips so I could run many of my own errands.

I suppose the major downside of the dorms was the community bathroom. Naturally, I didn't want Ashley to wait right outside my toilet stall every time I used the restroom, but if she went back to our room down the hall, there was no way for me to tell her when I was finished. So sometimes I would just tell her to come back in 10 minutes. Some of those times I was done in five minutes and would have to wait around, and some of those times Ashley would get busy doing something and would come in a few minutes late and so I would have to wait around even more. It got really old not being able to just get off the toilet when I was finished.

The shower arrangement also got a little tricky. Most of the shower stalls had a curtain that separated a small space to dress in and then had another curtain separating the actual shower. The accessible shower only had one curtain though, that went right into the shower. For a few weeks, I would drive my wheelchair into the stall where I would undress and Ashley would transfer me to my bath chair. Then Ashley would drive my wheelchair out of the shower while I bathed and then back in again when I was finished. This process was very time consuming though, and being that we were college students who stayed up late at night and couldn't get out of bed in the morning, we decided we needed a faster approach.

In the mornings when I would get up, I used the restroom first, and it would certainly be a waste of time to pull my pants back on just to take them off again in two seconds when I got to the shower. So, I would make a run for it from the toilet stall to the shower stall with no pants or underwear on, just a T-shirt pulled down to somewhat cover me. Then, we would look around and make sure no one was in the restroom, or that if there was someone, that they were at least occupied in a stall, and Ashley would just pick me up and carry me into the shower stall, cutting at least five minutes off of our routine. I just hoped no one ever got a peek at my vulnerable moment. Talk about embarrassing.

I also felt bad about waking Ashley up a couple of times in the middle of the night, every night, to turn me. At home, I would usually wake my dad up first, and then if I needed to turn again I would call for my mom. This way, each of my parents' REM's were only interrupted once. With Ashley though, she was it. Although waking up twice is the norm, there were always the nights when I would sleep all night, never needing any help. There were also nights though, when I was restless. My restlessness inevitably equals someone else's restlessness. On nights when I wanted to turn frequently, usually waking up with my knees painfully pressing up against each other, or if on my back, my tail bone sore from the bed, I would often lay there, watching the clock, buying minutes to space out the intervals so that Ashley could get just a few more minutes of sleep.

After a few weeks, Ashley got my routine down, and was able to get me comfortable in bed. She told me once that after she put me in bed, she got into her bed, got comfortable, and then laid there unmoving, trying to fall asleep. She knew that every night when she put me in bed, that was my position for the next few hours, and she wanted to see if she could fall asleep in her initial position too. She did not succeed. Ashley, like most people, had to toss and turn many times before falling asleep and was in awe that I could fall asleep without the ability to first reposition several times. Luckily, I have ascertained the world's most comfortable bed and I now rarely need help turning at night.

Despite being very old, the campus was mostly accessible. There were some buildings that did not have automated doors, and I would have to find someone to help me get inside (which was horrible when it was cold or rainy because I would have to sit outside until someone walked by), but for the most part I could get around independently. The UT campus is huge, but it was easy for me to get around in my electric wheelchair. Other than having to meet Ashley every few hours to use the restroom, I was on my own.

As far as classes were concerned, I tried to remain as independent as possible. It was nice living on campus because I could use the dorm room as a base camp. I did not want to carry my books in a backpack because that meant I would always have to ask people to help me all day long. Instead, I just carried what I needed at the time, on my lap. The first day of classes was always a little scary because I would not know the layout of the rooms, or the location of the accessible seats. While many of my classes were in huge stadium seating classrooms, with the accessible seating in the back near the door, other classrooms were smaller, had two doors, only one of which did not have steps, with accessible seating in the very front. So I would have to figure out which door I needed to go in, and then find someone to open it for me. Then I would have to sit in the very front, which always made me feel very uncomfortable. I am sure there are a lot of people who don't like to sit in the front for various reasons, but for me, I think it was just the fact that people have always stared at me, and I felt on display at the front of the room. There were some small classrooms that had individual seats that were nailed into the floor, with very little free space. Although I had to ask to have the entire class moved on one occasion because there was literally no place for me to sit, sometimes there was room to put a table for me at the front corner of the room. In that situation, I was at the front, a few feet from the professor, and I could hardly even read what was written on the chalkboard because of the angle I was sitting at. Every day a student would have to slide my table over so that I could get behind it, and then push it back in front of me.

As a result of the curvature of my spine that still affects the way I sit, even after my back surgeries, most of my weight sits on my right leg. So, my right leg falls asleep all day long, every day. There is very little blood flow into my leg and it is painful. This explains why every few minutes I have to lean over, because when I do so, I can feel the blood go into my leg and it makes the pain go away until I have to lean again. During class, I would often lean my head on my hand, to the left, in order to relieve my right leg. It was a very comfortable position, but it was hard to sit like that if my desk was on the right side of the room because I would basically have my head turned away from the professor.

One semester, I had a class with a discussion group that was held once a week, and being the second week of class, I had only gone once. I left my dorm and made the 15 minute journey to the building my class was in. I pushed the up button to call the elevator, and then I realized that I had no idea what room my class was in, or even what floor it was on. I looked for a phone to call my roommate so she could look it up for me, but I was unable to find one. I knew that if I went all the way back to my dorm to find out where my class was, the class would be over by the time I got back.

There was a male student walking down the hall towards me, and suddenly I had an idea. I stopped him and asked him if he had a few minutes, to which he responded that he did. I told him that I could not remember where my class was, but I knew it was in this building, and I knew what my TA looked like, but I was too short to see into the windows on the classroom doors. This stranger then went down the hall with me, describing the professors he saw in each window. He described someone as fat, and I said nope, that's not him. Then someone had glasses...that wasn't him. Before I knew it we had done the whole floor and had not found my classroom. I apologized for his time, but the student was very generous and suggested we try another floor. When we got into the elevator and he asked me what floor, I told him to pick one, his guess was as good as mine.

Finally, we came to a window where the description fit my TA. I didn't want to just barge in the wrong class though, especially since I was now 15 minutes late. I can not exactly slide in the door and inconspicuously take my seat. I asked him if he could see anything written on the board. He told me there were a bunch of Ts and Fs. I then knew it was the right class; I was taking symbolic logic and we were learning how to do truth tables. He opened the door for me.

The dorm I lived in had its own cafeteria, and while the food could have been better, it was certainly convenient. I would usually eat with girls that lived in my hall, and Ashley. We would all go to the cafeteria entrance, line up to swipe our meal cards, and then make our way to get our trays and silverware. Like any other time I am walking with people, sometimes we would walk too close to each other, and it is inevitable that sometimes a toe would sneak under a wheel. Although I always hate it when I run people over, naturally feeling guilty for causing someone pain, I really feel uncomfortable when it happens in front of a lot of people because it perpetuates the closed vision that results in seeing me as a wheelchair. As we walked into the cafeteria, there were people sitting all around, and if we ran into each other, I would just hope my friends would not make a scene.

I knew people in high school too that found my running over them adequate reason to be dramatic. I always appreciated the people, when getting a toe squished, would say "ouch" and move on. The others, who would freak out, would make everyone stare at us (like I needed any help in that area), and I always felt embarrassed. I wasn't a student. I was a machine that hurt people. WATCH OUT!

One particular time in college, I ran over my friend Nicole on the way in to the cafeteria and she made somewhat of a scene. I had certainly seen worse, but later that evening I was telling her and Ashley how that embarrassed me. They understood while at the same time thought I was a little weird.

The next day Ashley came home from her individual differences class, where they had been studying disability, and she had just experienced something very interesting that reinforced what I had been telling her just the night before. In small groups, the students were discussing experiences they had had with people who had disabilities. One of the students in Ashley's group told everyone that there was one girl at his high school that had been in a wheelchair. The only other thing he said about it was, "She used to run everyone over all the time." Ashley told me after hearing that, she understood what I meant.

My first year at UT, Dana was finishing his last year. It was nice knowing he was there, I didn't really know anyone when I moved to Austin. He came over to the dorm and ate with me a few times each week and we went to a play once and out to dinner another time. In the fall, Dana asked me to go to his Navy formal, the very one that he had missed my prom for the year before. I was honored to have the invitation.

When Dana picked me up, I actually drove (his formal happened to be during one of the few weeks I was driving my van), he looked better than I'd ever seen him. It's amazing what a uniform will do for a guy. I looked pretty good myself, if I do say so...he thought so too although all I could get out of him was, "You look great...you look so mature."

I had heels on my shoes and when I got into the van, my knees were too high to fit under the steering apparatus, and Dana had to slip my shoes off for me to drive. I thought his gentle touch on my ankle would make me faint. Was I deprived of the sensation of being touched by a male?

The night was wonderful and I was disappointed when he escorted me home. Why couldn't I tell him how I felt? Was it because he was four years older than me? So is my dad...to my mom. Was it that he knew me from camp? I knew that he saw me as more than just a camper. Was it because I felt so young from my sexual inexperience compared to he who had lived with a girlfriend once? I didn't feel sexually immature. In fact the evening when he lovingly brushed his finger on my cheek as we walked down the hall toward my room, I felt anything but sexually immature. There is no way he ever had any feelings for me, even remotely. Why would he? Did I find myself analyzing everything he said to me? I'm sorry to say I did. I felt so much for him and was so afraid, insecure to ever tell him so I searched, searched for something that would indicate to me that maybe I wasn't completely alone in my feelings. I didn't want anything from him. I never wanted to be his girlfriend. I think I was looking more for an assurance that I could find a beautiful man who I cared for deeply, who could be attracted to me. Please, just a little.

Maybe over the eight years I had known him, perhaps he felt attracted to me once, for a moment, but if so, I never knew it. When Lauren flew in to Austin from California to spend a long weekend with me on campus, I told him that I wanted him to meet her. For some reason he thought that was strange and never did meet up with us. That, on top of the several times he stood me up (although he usually had a good excuse like a broken foot from soccer practice), and the one too many times I found myself crying over him, all amounted to a feeling of bitterness; yet without any love interests in my life, I found it difficult to move on. I didn't even see him before he left for California to join the Navy. I never said goodbye. Neither did he. I do hear from him even now, once and awhile, usually through email. He is a Navy Seal. Thankfully, as I knew I eventually would, I finally moved on.

The summer after my first year in college, my parents and I took a road trip to Washington D.C. We didn't want to deal with the airlines, and we wanted to have reliable transportation in Washington, so we decided to just drive. We had taken road trips before; we had actually made the drive to Chicago several times. The only difficulties with driving are finding accessible restrooms to stop at on the way, and finding accessible places to sleep. We had made all the arrangements for Washington, and we had an accessible room waiting for us there, but we hadn't made plans for the road since we weren't exactly sure how far we would be traveling each day, and where we would be spending the night.

After driving all day, we knew we couldn't wait until late to find a room for the night, because hotels fill up fast, and especially the two rooms each hotel has that are accessible. Even at 9:00 the first night, we had a difficult time finding somewhere to sleep. We were in a small town, and the first two places we stopped did not have any accessible rooms left that had two beds. The third place, and the last in that town, gave us the key to an accessible room. When we pulled our van around, we realized that the doorway to the room they had given us was up a step a foot and a half tall, not a good sign.

My parents went into the room, and the only thing that made it accessible was a bar in the bathroom, attached to the wall. The bathroom had a narrow door and was too small for my wheelchair anyway. The sink had cabinets all underneath it, making it unusable for me as well. We knew that if we kept driving, the lack of available rooms would only get worse as it got later, and we decided to just make the room work for one night. It was quite a challenge to get my wheelchair into the room, and out the next morning. I didn't even bother trying to shower.

The bathroom situation while driving wasn't much better. After driving for hours and stopping at a rest area, and knowing there wasn't another rest area for at least another 45 minutes, I was willing to do whatever it took to make the bathroom work. One of the places we stopped had an accessible stall, indicated by the raised toilet and the bars on the wall, but it was the regular width, and there was nowhere for my wheelchair. I parked my wheelchair out in the open, propping the stall door open, my mom pulled down my pants out in the public area, carried my naked ass into the restroom, and I did everything with the door open. Sometimes there is no room for modesty.

The capital of our country was very accessible. We enjoyed a week of relaxation and learned quite a bit at the various tourist attractions, all without frustration. It was one of the few vacations we have taken, which was spent as a vacation should be.

Years earlier, at MDA camp, the woman who was at that time the director of MDA, brought her son to camp for the week. Dennis was younger than I was (I was twelve at the time), but we spent a lot of time together that week. He basically just ran around doing whatever he wanted all week, and much of that time was spent with me. We had a good time, and laughed a lot, but I remember everyone giving me a hard time because everyone said he had a crush on me. I didn't think much of it.

Six years later, the summer after my first year in college, Dennis came back to camp, this time as a volunteer...he was finally sixteen, the minimum age required to be an attendant. Angela had told me beforehand that she had heard he was coming, and I have to admit I was looking forward to seeing him again. When I first saw him that week it was a little awkward, like we knew each other, because we did, just not the way we were now...no longer in middle school. By the end of the week we had talked several times and his personality was attracting me. I knew I was nineteen and he wouldn't be seventeen for two months, but it didn't stop me from being attracted to him. I was also pretty sure he felt the same way about me too.

As is tradition, there was a huge party the night we got back from camp. Dennis called me the afternoon we got home, needing a ride to the party, and Stacey agreed that we could pick him up on our way. Ashley, my college roommate, who also volunteered at camp, went with us too.

150

The party was nothing special; everyone hung out and drank all night. I saw Dennis a few times, but that was it. On the way home, Dennis was sitting in the back seat of the van, a little behind where I sit in my wheelchair, and somehow I found my hand in his, his thumb caressing my skin with tenderness I had never known before. As childish and innocent a move as it may seem, it sent sensations through my nineteen year old, sexually deprived body, that gave me chills. After spending a year in college, hormones out of control, lonely, wanting love, wanting to be touched, he was making me feel like a woman for the first time in my life. Not wanting it to end, we eventually got to his house and he got out of the van; not a word was spoken. It was a deep, lasting touch.

We talked all summer, mostly for hours late at night. At times I was frustrated because I could tell the difference just a few years in age made. We had some really nice talks though. Even so, it wasn't meant to be, he was so young and I was so far away at school, but despite the fact that more of a relationship never developed, I'll never forget the way he made me feel that night. It doesn't happen often. We are still friends to this day and he even accompanied me to a wedding that I was a bridesmaid in. At the wedding he was kind enough to put up with my crazy dancing for the entire night! Apparently I like to spin.

15

Before I knew it, I was back in the dorms, starting my second year of college. I was glad to be back, and I certainly enjoy being away at school, but I am pretty sure college means something different for me than it does for the majority of students. Although I stay busy with classes and volunteer work, my social life will never be that of an average college student.

Sure, there are always things going on, but most of them I can not be a part of. Parties, for one thing, are usually not part of my plans. They are always held at apartment complexes, and of course, are rarely on the first floor. Either that or they are at frat houses, not too accessible either.

My friend Melissa was a part of a campus organization that was having a party at a club downtown one night. She invited Ashley and I, but not having transportation, we walked from 26th street where we lived, to 6th street where the party was. When we got down there, we discovered that the party was up a flight of stairs. We couldn't get to it, so, we walked home.

My friends also liked to go country dancing, and this made me feel very left out. There was a short time when they were going every week, talking about it before hand, talking about what they were going to wear, and bringing back stories that night. They never invited me along, just assuming I couldn't participate, and my feelings were very hurt. I finally had to talk to them about it. They told me they hadn't ever asked me because it was so crowded that I could never go. I didn't understand why they couldn't find a place we could all go dancing, after all, I was their friend too. They didn't go for awhile after that, someone was always too busy or didn't feel like going, but they still make tentative plans often and Nicole especially continued to tell me how long it had been since they had gone and how she really wanted to go. I guess my feelings weren't really listened to; maybe my request was just too big.

The things we did together usually consisted of the routine grocery shopping or frequent trips to Walmart. These trips usually ended with us having some funny story to tell. Like the one time we went to Walmart and I decided I wanted to buy a fish to go in my dorm room. I was holding my fish in its little plastic bag, going through the store, probably with a grin because of my excitement, when an employee of Walmart passed me and said "Hey there Hotrod!" I suppose I was asking for it. I'm sure I looked like a moron alright with that fish and the excitement on my face. I looked over at my friends and they just smiled.

We went to the grocery store one night at about 10:00, and our trip ended in quite the adventure. On the way back to the dorm, our van hit a bump, and for just a second the lights went off on the dashboard and the radio stopped, and then everything went back to normal. So we thought. We parked the van in the parking lot behind the dorm, undid the straps holding my wheelchair down, and then found out that the lift was dead. I was in my wheelchair, in the van, and could not get out. There was no way my girlfriends would have been able to lift my wheelchair either. It always took four men to lift a wheelchair into the semi truck that carried everyone's wheelchairs to camp, and even they struggled. Then all of the girls that lived in our hall started coming outside, and somehow they got the idea into their head that we should call the firemen to come help us. They were all ranting and raving about the calendar with all the hot firemen they had seen, and they were ready to call. I had to calm them down, telling them that in reality all firemen do not look like that, and there was no way I was having a fire truck with all the commotion come rescue me. I called a couple of my strong guy friends, and they were able to get my wheelchair out for me. Then we got the lift fixed.

Sometimes we also went to the movie theater, but that form of entertainment became much less enjoyable for me when all of the new movie theaters being built started to have stadium seating. People who use wheelchairs were REALLY being thought of when architects were drafting what would become the design of every movie theater in the country.

All of the wheelchair seating is now in the front of the theater, the most desirable and fought over seats available. Why are they so popular, you may be asking? Well, probably because you have to look straight up to see the screen, straining your neck and your eyes, and all of the characters on screen are short and squatty from your skewed perspective. While the seats in these theaters are tall so people can rest their heads and lean back, and while I have a headrest and layback mechanism that allows me to lean back in my wheelchair, most people in wheelchairs have to sit in these front row seats with no support for their neck while they look straight up for two hours.

Even with the features on my wheelchair, the view I have is not desirable, and I am furious that many people can't go to the movies at all anymore. Before the thousands of new theaters were built, it would have been nice if someone actually sat, in a wheelchair, in a designated spot and watched a two hour long movie like that. Then, maybe, a little more consideration would have been given.

Friendly people are awesome. It always put me in a good mood when I was on my way to class and a stranger would say hi or smile. When someone would tell me to stop speeding and then chuckle, or when they would threaten to give me a ticket, I smiled because I knew they were just friendly people trying to make a joke. I encountered such comments weekly, even all over a college campus, including in my dorm, where it was obvious that I am intelligent enough to be a college student. But since this is my book, and I can say whatever I want, I can finally admit that I don't think it's funny. AT ALL. Despite this, I am sure I will continue to smile, knowing that such lame comments are often the result of discomfort and an inability to relate to me. At least they are trying.

After living in the dorms for a year, my roommate, Ashley, and I were ready to move into an apartment. Although the dorms were convenient, allowing us to sleep until the last possible minute before rushing across campus to class, we were ready for our own rooms. The dorm room was small, just enough room for two beds and two desks and a few other pieces of furniture. The room had it's own sink, but we were ready to have our own bathroom. As much as the companionship was nice, having to share a room with someone can get old at times. You never have your own space, and so the other person's needs and wants always need to be taken into consideration, whether watching TV, listening to the radio, sleeping, or studying.

My second year in college Ashley and I got a dorm room once again deciding that we would make use of its convenience for another year, but that we would search early for an accessible apartment for the following year.

During the fall semester of my second year, Ashley and I found two people who wanted to get an apartment with us. It was important to me that we find a four bedroom apartment and go in on it with several girls because I knew that I would need a few people around. Although Ashley was my only attendant, I constantly asked for help from girls that lived near me in the dorm. Inevitably there would be times when Ashley wasn't home and I would need help with something, whether it was opening a container that held my lunch, or picking up something I had dropped. One semester Ashley had a morning class hours earlier than I did, and I would stay in bed until she got back from class. Several times during that semester though I had needed something, either to go to the bathroom or was not comfortable. I would just call my neighbors on the phone and they would come and help. Or what about the night when Ashley was studying in the lounge and for some reason couldn't hear me calling for her, so I just banged on the wall next to my bed until I woke up Melissa and she came half asleep into my room? In an apartment setting I knew that I would not be able to go knock on people's doors as easily, asking for help. I figured if I lived with three other girls, most of the time, someone would probably be home. In the instances when no one would be home I would just have to set up everything that I would need when everyone was gone, much like I did during the summers at home when both of my parents were at work all day.

So the four of us set out to find an accessible, four bedroom apartment. We were all very excited about having our own rooms and a kitchen (which meant no more dorm cafeteria food), even a living room with a couch. We spent much of our time planning the things we would need, and who would be able to bring what. Katie, one of the girls we were to live with, was a friend of Ashley's and mine. Ashley and Katie had the same major and so had many of their classes together. Although they had known each other in the past, we saw much more of Katie that year because she lived down the hall from us. Nicole, the other person who we were going to live with, we had known for a year since she lived on our hall the previous year too.

We decided to go to an apartment search agency to help us find what we were looking for. When we sat down with the agent, he basically told us that we were not going to find what I was looking for, as far as accessibility was concerned, anywhere near campus. He told us that all of the apartment complexes in the city were very old and that there were not many guidelines for construction when they were built. Many of them did not offer any accessible apartments, and he said that the ones that did were barely accessible. My hopes of finding an apartment with a bathroom sink that I could roll under, for instance, he said would be unlikely. He then recommended that we consider two apartment complexes in particular that were only two years old and so were very likely quite accessible. The only downside was that those apartments were much farther away from campus than we hoped to be, a ten or fifteen minute drive in no traffic, they were about a forty five minute bus ride away, at least.

That brought me to the next problem. I was very anti-public transportation. For one thing, I swore I would never ride the bus again after I finally became free from needing its use when I graduated high school. The past year was so wonderful being completely independent, being able to go to class, or meetings, or run errands, all on my own. I knew that riding a bus would strip me from some of that independence. I knew if I rode the bus I would have to put my headrest on my wheelchair. Since I am unable to place the headrest on the back of my seat, and I did not want to go around campus all day with it on, I would have to ask the bus driver to take it on and off. I knew that would be an awkward situation. The driver would also have to strap down my wheelchair to the bus, and I had heard stories about their reluctance to do so correctly if they wanted to hurry and keep the bus route on time. I had also seen the way the buses stopped around campus, and not only was I concerned about how my back would feel from the bumps on the road that are only made worse on a huge bus, but I was worried that I would not have enough upper body strength to hold myself up when they were stopping. Also, like in high school, I would not be able to get my books in and out of my backpack and so I would have to hold them on my lap. While this is fine when I am just rolling around on campus, surely I would have dropped them all over the floor of the campus bus just as I often did in high school on my little yellow bus.

Overall, I guess you could say that I did not want to ride the bus, at least not on a regular basis. I especially felt that way because I had a van with a lift on campus, and I wanted to make use of it. Although parking was a major problem for any student who drove a car to campus, I escaped that problem because I could park in handicapped parking anywhere on campus.

When we first realized that we were going to most likely be getting an apartment far from campus, I went to Nicole and talked to her about driving me to school. Nicole was the only person left from the year before who felt comfortable driving my van. At UT, scheduling classes was always hard, because there were more students than spaces available in classrooms, and so it was always a race to get the classes you wanted. Ashley and I, along with other disabled students, were allowed to register early, when all of the classes were still available so that we could coordinate our schedules. I had informed Nicole that she would be able to register early with me too, as my second attendant, and that we could coordinate most of our classes so it would be convenient for her to drive me to campus. After all, it would be nice for her too not to have to ride the bus. I understood that she wouldn't want to have to wait around for me if I had a class and she didn't, but I was willing to wait around for her if it meant I wouldn't have to ride the bus, and so I figured we would be able to work something out, at least for most of the days of the week. So we agreed and nothing more was really said about it.

About a month later we all decided to go look at the actual apartment since that would be the only way I would really know it was accessible and then we would find out when we needed to sign a contract. We went into the office of the first complex and they informed us that they only had double apartments that were accessible, not four bedroom. Then we went across the street to the other apartment complex. The lady who was working said that they did have four bedroom accessible apartments but she wasn't exactly sure how they were laid out and what features they had to make it accessible. She also did not have a unit that she could show me. There was no way that I was going to sign a contract and make living arrangements based on their idea of accessibility without first seeing it with my own eyes. I asked the lady which apartment numbers the four bedroom accessible ones were, and then the girls and I went knocking on their door. Someone opened the door and we told her that we had a very strange request but that she had an accessible apartment and I wanted to take a look at it to see if it would work out for me. The person who lived there was very nice and agreed to let us in. I first glanced at the kitchen which was so small that my wheelchair wouldn't really fit in it; I wasn't even sure if I would be able to get at the refrigerator. We then took a look at the bathroom. I became very concerned when I saw that there were cabinets all along the underside of the sink. I had visions of brushing my teeth next to the sink in the kitchen at our old house, and utilizing the sink in this situation would be impossible because of the dimensions. Then the door leading into the bathroom where the toilet and shower were was swinging in. I would not be able to take my wheelchair into the bathroom, which meant I would have to undress outside of the restroom and be carried in. This, the supposedly most accessible apartment I was going to find, was not very accessible at all.

We left the apartment complex and headed back to the dorm, and I was less than elated about the situation. I knew it was the best we were going to find, and with some work it would make due, but life was certainly going to be harder than it had been in the dorms. It didn't matter though, I was sick of living in the dorms and I was willing to make the sacrifice, but I didn't have to be excited about it. Sacrificing ones needs is never really exciting.

Well, apparently my bad attitude was making the girls distraught. I could tell that they were talking about me behind my back because they each kept making random remarks that told me they obviously were having

161

conversations about me. I'm not an idiot, and I could tell. So they each started telling me pieces, bit by bit, small parts of the conversations coming from all of the girls. The comments ranged from concerns about my being happy in the apartment and they didn't want to have to be around me if I was unhappy, to Nicole complaining that my transportation was going to be her sole responsibility and she didn't how she got into that situation, to Katie wanting to know how much she was going to have to do for me if I lived with them, ending with concerns that I couldn't cook for myself and they would have to do it. At that time, Katie and I did not know each other very well yet, and I knew that she was getting nervous just from hearing Ashley and Nicole's comments. Of course, though, no one was coming to me with these concerns and instead they were talking about me behind my back. I started to feel sick to my stomach when I thought about a living situations where concerns were handled that way, and I knew it would only get worse. I thought that if I was feeling like that then, that I should listen to my gut before I signed any lease.

All this happened Wednesday and Thursday, and Thursday evening Nicole was driving the two of us back to Houston for the weekend. I decided not to bring it up with everyone, instead I just wanted to go home, get a break, and think about it with a clear head. Although I planned on just talking about it with my parents, Nicole and I started talking about it on our two hour drive back to Houston. I told her about everything I knew that was being said about me and how everyone's worries were just making me feel like a huge burden. I told her I didn't want to have to feel like a burden, and I also didn't want to live with people who were not able to confront me with their concerns. Then, after knowing Nicole for a year, she disclosed some information that she had no idea would change the way I saw her from then on.

162

We were talking about friendships and she told me that she felt like in our friendship she was just giving and giving and giving, and then she just had to realize that she was getting a wonderful friend in return. I suppose by her saying "and then I realize," she thought it was okay that she was telling me that, but it wasn't okay at all. What was she giving and giving and giving? Crossing my leg for me? Opening a can of tuna? Helping me put on a coat if it was cold outside? I had no idea she felt so put out by these requests that I had always seen as being so insignificant.

It didn't end there. About a week before, Ashley and her boyfriend Benny were planning on going to a party and I wasn't able to go with them because it was in an upstairs apartment with no elevator. I knew they were going to be out pretty late and so I had gone to Nicole and asked her if she had any plans for Saturday night. I told her Ashley and Benny were going out and I thought we could go see a movie or rent one or something. She told me that sounded good and that was that. On the way home, Nicole confessed to me that after that conversation she had gone back to her room and started to become angry that I was going to be her responsibility that night and now she wasn't going to be able to go out and do anything. She again concluded with, "but then I realized you are just my friend trying to make plans for the night." I could not believe it. The fact that she would ever even think such things saddened me. Even after we had been friends for a year, she obviously was not seeing me for who I am.

So that night I got home and I started to tell my parents what had been happening over the past few days, and I became very upset. I was unhappy about the plans I had for a living arrangement for the following year, but I felt trapped and without options. I didn't know of anyone else who needed roommates and I certainly did not want to live in the dorms again. Furthermore, I knew it was hard on both Ashley and I that she was my only attendant. She could never stay gone for an extended amount of time because I needed to use the restroom about every six hours or so. She could never spend the night at a friend's house or go home for the weekend unless I had a ride to go home too, because I needed her help. It was a large overall responsibility, especially for someone in college. It was a lot like having a child I suppose, where everything you do you have to think about the implications it will have on your child. I didn't think our relationship was growing to be very healthy either. Though it was largely due to my insecurities, I was beginning to feel a real imbalance of power between us. She knew that I desperately needed her and there was no one else to help and there were certainly times when knowing she was aware of the situation, I felt my behavior was altered. It was not really anything in particular Ashley was doing, but rather a feeling that we both knew that she could really do whatever she wanted because I would not be able to fire her. I wondered if it was possible for any human to be needed so much by another and never be negatively affected by that? Lastly, I was very upset about the way Nicole was seeing me. I had never had a friend that felt that way about me and I didn't really want to have that dysfunction in my life. I knew I couldn't talk to her about it because it would be pointless. She would naturally only get defensive, and make excuses, and I knew I wouldn't be able to change who she was.

My parents and I needed to come up with some sort of a plan. I still had several years of college left, and I knew I could not continue doing what I had been doing for the rest of my time there. It was very difficult being so far away from my parents too. It wasn't like I had my own transportation and could just come home whenever I wanted. I could only leave when it was convenient for someone to take me back to Houston, and my parents were getting tired of making the drive. For them to come pick me

164

up for the weekend, they would have to work all day, leave work and drive two hours to come pick me up, get me, then turn around and drive back for two hours, to do the same thing two days later when I had to go back. Needless to say, I didn't get to go home as much as I would have liked.

So that weekend, after many tears were shed, we came up with a few conclusions. My parents were tired of living out in Katy where they had to drive forever to get anywhere. My father was not going anywhere in his career, and company policies were driving him to find a new job. My mother was very unhappy in her job, had been wanting to quit for years, and was getting closer and closer to the edge. Her stress level at work on top of the three hours she spent in traffic each day were too much. I needed another support system at school; I felt emotionally exhausted from Nicole and from having to physically depend solely on Ashley. And, my parents loved Austin, much more than Houston. So we decided that weekend, that there was one clear solution to everyone's problems: my parents were going to move to Austin.

Ever since I had gone to college, there wasn't really any reason left for my parents to stay in the suburbs; school districts weren't an issue anymore. They had been looking for a house closer to the city for about a year. All of the older homes were either not accessible or way too expensive to be able to afford to make the necessary changes, like putting in ramps and widening doorways. They had also looked at buying a lot in the city and building a house, but the price of the land was so expensive close to the city that they could not have afforded to build much of a house by the time they paid for the lot. It seemed now there was a very good reason why they had been unable to find a place to move to. If they had recently moved in closer to Houston, they would not have been in a position to transfer to Austin.

The search for a used home in Austin was just as frustrating as it had been in Houston. All of the homes in our price range would have needed so many modifications to make it accessible that they were no longer in our price range. We didn't really want to have to spend a lot of money on those types of things anyway, because while they would make the house livable for me, those types of changes do not increase the value of the home at all and so as far as resale is concerned, it's like flushing thousands of dollars down the toilet. At the point of extreme discouragement, we found our way, quite arbitrarily, to a lot for sale. This lot in particular had the features we had only dreamed of, and it was at a price my parents could afford to build on. There it was, we finally found a place to live.

Ashley and I also found out about a new dorm that was being built, a dorm where each room would have its own bathroom, and where the accessible rooms would be the size of one and a half of the other rooms. We knew that was the place for us.

As a member of the President's Committee for Student's with Disabilities on campus, I was present when the accessibility of the new dorm was being discussed. When the building was first planned, every room was designed with the ADA guidelines of door width in mind. This way, students who used wheelchairs would be able to visit friends in other rooms and even be able to fit their wheelchair through the bathroom door in each room. Somehow though, as plans progressed, it was discovered that the slab for the building was not quite long enough, and the "people in charge" had gotten a waiver to ignore the ADA guideline, making the bathroom door entries to non-accessible rooms too small for a wheelchair. The few inches this freed up in each room was enough to solve the problem. So, basically, it isn't too big of a deal...if I am in a friend's room and need to use the restroom I will just have to go back to my room. There is a bigger issue at stake. In the year 2000, a brand new building with all the opportunity of being completely accessible was poorly planned and the very first thing to go was wheelchair accessibility. The first thing.

16

About the middle of the semester I took my first essay test. In high school I had written essays in my English class, and I had never needed extended time. Although I had never taken an essay test in a college class, I was not concerned. I should have been. After frantically writing for fear of running out of time, for an hour and fifteen minutes with no break, I was so weak that I could hardly move. I turned in my test with what little iota of strength I had left and I told my professor I could never do that again; I was so weak that my neck could barely hold up my head.

I spoke with Mike over at the Services for Students with disabilities office, and he told me that many students need extended time and that there was nothing wrong with getting test taking accommodations. Although he tried to dissuade me, I couldn't help but feel like getting extra time would detract from the quality of the work that could be given credit to me. It wouldn't be fair. Even though I was much weaker than my classmates, and it took much more effort on my part to write for that long, extra time would help me to do better. The gratification I received when I got an "A" would not be as great if I had different test taking circumstances than the people I was competing with.

A few weeks later I got my grade back. I had been given a 98 on a test where the average score was well below that. It practically killed me, but I did it, and it felt that much better because it had been such a struggle.

I am a good student, and I study often, but not in the libraries. I hate going to libraries because of my wheelchair.

My motor always seems so loud in the silence of everyone studying, and many heads look up as I pass.

One night, I didn't have a choice though, I needed a few books for a research paper I was doing. I had never been to the particular library I was going to, and as I entered the elevator to go up to the floor where the library was located, I hoped I would be able to reach the buttons and be strong enough to push them in. Every new elevator I use is a little scary because I never know if I will be able to operate the buttons, and I don't find out until I am inside with the door shut, a little too late to do anything if I can't.

The elevator at the library worked well though, and soon I had distracted everyone studying, retrieved the materials I needed, and was on my way. When I got back into the elevator, there was a large, hard plastic sheet leaning up against the wall. It looked kind of like a cover for a florescent light. I had to push up against it to get at the elevator buttons, and when the elevator door opened at my floor, it fell on me as I backed up to get off. Being as afraid of getting stuck in elevators as I am, my immediate reaction was to floor it, getting out of the elevator at whatever it took. The plastic thing banged against my wheelchair, but I was able to escape.

I headed back home, to my dorm, and just before I was to cross the street in front of my building, my wheelchair stopped working. The screen on my joystick read some technical mumbo jumbo, and all I understood was that there was a problem with my right motor. I stopped a stranger who was also waiting to cross the street, and asked her to fidget with the lever that I pointed to, which was connected to my right motor. She popped it right back into place and my chair started running again. That plastic sheet had knocked loose the switch used to disconnect my motor, and I guess every bump I hit in the sidewalk knocked it looser and looser until it completely popped out. It's a good thing I wasn't in a desolate area.

One night, I went to bed at about one thirty in the morning, I had been studying for a test the next day but then got too tired and decided to quit. At four thirty I woke up with a stomach ache. I woke up my roommate and told her I needed to use the restroom. We got out of bed and walked down the hall to our community bathroom. Ashley put me on the toilet and I told her to come back in five minutes. After five minutes, my stomach was feeling okay, and I wasn't feeling as nauseous. I figured my feeling sick probably had something to do with the café mocha, popcorn, trail mix, and chocolate candy I had eaten shortly before going to bed. As I sat on the toilet, five minutes came and went, so did twenty, then forty-five. I was panicking. At this point I knew that my roommate had fallen back asleep. What I didn't know was if she had been completely awake when we had gone to the bathroom. If not, she would never even know I was missing. I thought maybe she was in a dreamy state and just went back to the room and got into bed, completely forgetting that I was in the bathroom. I just hoped that maybe she would snap awake and realize I wasn't there. An hour passed. I started to scream for help, calling for the two girls whose room was adjacent to the bathroom. I knew one of the girls slept with ear plugs, and that the other was a heavy sleeper, but I called for them anyway, for thirty minutes. Then I started to cry as my legs were numbing and I could feel the lines on my thighs from the toilet seat. I turned on my wheelchair, which was within reach and drove it closer to me so that I could lean on the armrest, trying to bring some relief to my bottom. I started to become very angry; angry at the university housing for not having an accessible dormitory that also had an attached bathroom, where I would be able to call for Ashley when I was ready. Although such rooms existed, the only accessible ones with enough room for un-bunked beds had community bathrooms. Then I began to be angry with Ashley for allowing herself to fall asleep; how could she do that to me? As I cried, I thought of home and my parents, and I wished I were there, nothing like this would happen there. Each minute seemed like an eternity.

After an hour and a half had passed, and it was six fifteen in the morning, I knew that my salvation would soon come. Some people had eight o'clock classes and would be getting up at least within the next hour. I also knew that I had to get up at seven thirty and the time left for me to sleep was getting shorter. I was so cold, I was only wearing a t-shirt, and with no one in the showers to heat up the air, the bathroom was quite chilly. I kept hoping that someone would need to use the restroom in the middle of the night and they could go wake Ashley up, since I knew at that point she was sound asleep. I thought about how in a few hours I would be going to class and this would all be over. Then I thought about how helpless I was, how tired I was, and how much I wanted to cuddle up in bed. Then I began to cry again. I was worried that I was going to stop up the toilet with all the paper I was using to wipe my tears and blow my nose.

At six twenty five, I heard footsteps in the hall. My heart began to race, please God let them come into the restroom. I knew that if their footsteps began to fade I would scream out for help. Then the door opened, at last someone had come in for their morning shower. She went and got Ashley who came in with a look of shame on her face; she apologized and asked if I was okay. I replied no and we silently went back to bed. I had an hour left to sleep, a test in the morning, and I began to silently sob in bed. My bottom was sore, but after an hour and forty minutes spent trapped on the toilet, my realization of my situation and my dependence on others hurt me more.

In the morning, we spoke a little about it. I told Ashley that I wasn't angry and that I knew it had been an accident. She told me she had never been more sorry about anything in her life. After Ashley had left for class, but before I had to go to my own, I called my mom at work in Houston. I told her about what had happened and I was bawling on the phone. Of course she was so sorry that something like that ever had to happen to me. I was so sorry too. I went to class, took my test, and found myself biting my lip to keep from crying as I was coming home. When I got back to the dorm, Ashley was home and we started talking about it. We were both in tears as we realized that as dependable as she is, she is human and she made a mistake and unfortunately as much as I would always need people, sometimes they were going to make horrible mistakes that would cause me to suffer. I felt such a sorrowful depression as I thought about how dependent I was on others. It is such a helpless, frightening feeling. I think both of us were traumatized by that night. Surprisingly, we were both laughing about it hours later. Although I had thought to myself (among many other thoughts I had while sitting on that toilet) that I would never be able to laugh about this as I often laugh at my misfortunes, I did laugh and make jokes. Only, behind my laughter was a tinge of awareness of the frightening, cruel real world I had come to know just a little bit better.

My parents and I hadn't taken a family portrait since I was in third grade and we decided the time to get new ones done was already past due. I really wanted to have a recent picture taken of my family, and we thought they would make nice Christmas presents for everyone. We made an appointment at a photography studio at the new mall that had been built near our house.

When we got there, we all agreed that it would be nice for me to be out of my wheelchair, so that it would just be the three of us, al natural, in the pictures. I should have stayed in my wheelchair. Some of the poses had me on a stool, so rather than smiling when the photographer was clicking away, I was just trying not to fall off the stool. Instead of my parents lightly resting an arm on me, they were holding me up.

The other pictures had me sitting on a small box on the ground. Not only was this uncomfortable and difficult for me to keep my balance on, my parents had a hell of a time getting in the picture right too. We all had to sit close, but no one could knock me over. Then, my dad's back was about to break, lifting me on and off the floor to change positions and backdrops.

Of course, there had to be icing on our moist chocolate cake, so the photographer worked in front of a picture window where all of the strangers walking around in the mall could watch my rear end being lifted over and over again. Maybe that's why we only get portraits made once every ten years.

I have always hated it when people stare at me, and especially when I appear any less normal than I already do. I'll go around in my wheelchair and not feel embarrassed or ashamed at all, but the minute someone is picking me up, or carrying me, I don't want anyone to see. I always get mad when photographers take pictures of campers at MDA camp being lifted, and then use those pictures on TV for the Jerry Lewis Labor Day Telethon. No one wants the whole country to see them like that, ask anyone, those moments are personal.

There are other things too that I always make sure are right, so I am "normal." For instance, I have a headrest that I use in the car, and sometimes around the house. I will not go out in public with it on though. I may not be able to walk, but I can hold my own head up, and I don't want anyone thinking otherwise. Not that anyone would probably even notice my headrest. It kind of blends in with the rest of the package.

I also check in the mirror before I go out to be sure both of my pant legs are down evenly. Someone else puts them on me, and I would look ridiculous if one of my pant legs was five inches higher than the other one. It is important for me to be neatly kept. Since I have a disability, I feel like any blemish in my appearance would be blamed on my disability, and it is important to me that people see me as being similar to them, because I am. I don't want there to be any extra reasons for people to categorize me as being different than they are. I want to bridge that gap...I want people to look at me and think the only difference between her and me is that everything she does all day is done sitting down. Maybe it isn't that simple.

One semester I was asked to speak to a social work class at the University, along with a few other students with disabilities. Basically we told the students our personal story and then there was a question and answer session. Afterwards, several people approached me and thanked me for talking to them, mentioning some specific way that listening to us had helped their personal struggles. Not only was it wonderful to give some pointers to people who would be working with people with disabilities, but I became friends with one of the other people speaking that day. Megan had been in a car accident during her freshman year at UT and was paralyzed from the waist down. We talked some that day and exchanged phone numbers, but I really felt connected to her. We had things in common on a whole other level, and our personalities meshed well anyway.

One day we met for lunch, and after catching up on everything, I followed her back to her car. As I was driving my electric wheelchair next to her as she pushed her manual one, she asked me if I felt weird. We started laughing because we both felt so strange. People would walk by us, and it was just awkward. As much as I like her, and will continue to keep in touch with her, I know we won't ever become too close, it is just too weird for both of us to go around in public together. We are willing to ignore the double stares we get once and awhile and meet for lunch, but I doubt it will turn into more than that.

Megan really helped me though, in a way she doesn't even know. I often feel like guys don't ever look at me with interest, that I will never be the girl that some guy sees from across the room and would like to get to know. Whether I am on campus, or at a club on a Friday night, I don't feel attractive. It's not that I don't think I'm pretty, I just don't think anyone will ever be able to look at me and see past the wheelchair to notice that I am. Megan changed that. When I look at Megan, I think she is beautiful and that she would definitely be able to find some guy who thinks so. When I hear about her going on some date, or meeting some cutie, I realize though there aren't any guarantees, anything is possible.

My very dear friend Beth, whom I have known since I was 12, got married. I was honored when she asked me to be one of her bridesmaids. For a year, Beth was busy making preparations for her big day. We would talk constantly; Have you found a dress? Have you picked out the bridesmaids dresses? Can you believe you're getting married!?! It was an exciting time.

One of the first arrangements Beth made was a reception hall. She wanted to have it at a country club near her house, but she was unsure if there was a wheelchair accessible entrance. She had a long in-depth conversation with the woman who made the arrangements. Beth told her how heavy my wheelchair was, and that it could not be folded. She told her how important it was that I not have to get out of my wheelchair. Bottom line, was there a wheelchair lift or elevator? Yes. Perfect.

Months later while Beth was at the country club finalizing the plans, after the wedding invitations had been printed, she told the woman working with her (a different woman than the initial person who spoke with Beth) that she wanted to see the lift. She wanted to see how it worked and where exactly it was so everything would run smoothly on the day of her wedding. This woman gave Beth a puzzled look. What lift? Beth calmly reminded her that they had a lift they kept locked in a closet. The only thing the woman could think of was a contraption she unlocked and pulled out for Beth to look at. Beth went numb. It looked like an elementary school seat that would be manually pushed up a set of tracks used on the stairs. Not only was it unstable and scary, it did not provide a way for my wheelchair to get inside. Though the woman offered that they would carry me and my wheelchair, or let me use the manual wheelchair they had at their facility, Beth was infuriated. She had been completely misled and only she understood the significance of my needing to stay with my wheelchair during the reception.

She cried for days. I didn't even know about it. Beth didn't want to call me with the news until she had found a solution. Since the country club refused to install a lift for us, Beth's fiancé suggested they use a truck with a bobtail lift that they could get from the pool company he worked at to get me in. The loading dock at the back of the building provided an entrance on the level of the reception room and avoided the two flights of stairs that were the cause of the problem. We just needed a way to get me up the high concrete wall that opened up to the loading dock. With the truck, I could be lifted in my wheelchair to the loading dock and then enter the building through the kitchen. Beth called me with the problem, and the solution. I cried for having caused her such turmoil.

Beth was an exquisite bride and the wedding ceremony was beautiful. After plenty of pictures, we were all headed for the country club. When we pulled up to the loading dock, we discovered that it was at the top of a very steep hill. When we discovered that the man who was to back up this huge truck up this huge hill had never driven the truck before, we got a little nervous. When it took him 45 minutes to get it into position, almost crashing into everything and everyone, I was even more nervous. By this time we were gathering a crowd outside.

The truck was finally in position and it was time to let the lift down. Nobody could figure out how to release it. Someone went and got the groom because he was familiar with the lift. So here I was, pulling the groom away from his wedding, allowing him to tug on this dirty lift in his tuxedo, risking his back. They were leaving for a cruise the next day. I started to cry.

When the lift was finally lowered, it was not level with the ground. Since the truck was parked on a hill, with the back end up, when the lift was lowered, the back of it was also lifted up in the same angle as the truck. How was I going to get inside? Would I have to go home?

My mom (my parents had also been invited to the wedding) and I had already decided that there was no way in hell I was going to get on the back of the truck. Not if I wanted to live.

Someone brought a chair out onto the loading dock and my father lifted me in my dress and carried me up the steps.

There was no way the men would be strong enough to carry my wheelchair up the same steps, especially because the steps were so narrow and there would be nowhere for them to stand. Instead they lifted my wheelchair up the angle onto the lift of the truck. I friend of mine, Mark, who I had known from camp and who was friends with Beth, rode up the lift with my wheelchair. My father then told the driver to slowly back the truck up just a few feet so the lift could be lowered onto the dock. The next thing I knew, instead of slowly reversing, the truck was accelerating forward. My mother and I were both crying. The groom's father was trying to comfort us. I have never felt like a bigger burden. I was ruining Beth's wedding. Half of the wedding party was outside just trying to get me in. I didn't want to be so difficult, I didn't want any of this attention on her big day. No one should have had to help me inside, they should have been inside watching the bride. I was apologizing profusely. For what? My existence?

I shouldn't have had to apologize. The owner of the building who apparently felt a lift was unnecessary should have been outside apologizing. By the time I entered the building I was shaking. I had missed the grand entrance where the wedding party all entered in the same manner we walked down the aisle of the church. My name was never announced. I didn't get my food with the wedding party, instead I had to wait at the end of the line and ate alone. It didn't matter, when I actually sat down with my dinner, I realized I didn't have an appetite anyway. As I started to eat, Beth and her husband had their first dance. I was over an hour late.

I filed a lawsuit. They settled. A lift and many other accommodations are now installed.

17

As far as my future goes, I know that I want to continue my education. Whether I go for a PhD in psychology, or use my second major, philosophy, as a background in law school, I have to keep in mind, once again, who will be able to help me. Although graduate programs are highly competitive, I hope to be able to gain admission, whichever avenue I decide on, into the University of Texas. With my family moving to Austin, building a house to be accessible for me, they will not be in a position to move again, and I need to go to school where I have a network to assist me. Unlike other students, I will not be able to apply to 20 schools and go wherever I am accepted. It just isn't that simple.

I am determined to use the insight I have regarding disability in my career. I have seriously considered law school so that I can fight for the legal rights of people with disabilities. I'm pretty sure I feel strongly enough about such issues to spend my life working on them. Maybe I will go to graduate school for psychology and study perceptions of the general public on people with disabilities, or the impact disability has on families, or even individual self-esteem. Or I could work in a rehabilitation atmosphere helping people who have recently lost their mobility.

I have heard plenty of reports on job discrimination. This is farther down on my list of worries for the future, perhaps because looking for a job is further away on my timeline. I want to use my life experiences in my career, whether it is in law fighting for the rights of people with disabilities, or in psychology, working with people who have disabilities. In either career, I think I will be in a good place to avoid the kind of discrimination that is rumored to be more common practice in business and similar fields.

Who will care for me when my parents become too old to lift me anymore? What happens when most of my friends are married, and the pool of potential attendants gets smaller than it already is? Hopefully I'll find a wonderful man who will be willing to help me with many of my daily needs, or will be wealthy enough to hire someone to do so. If I do not meet that someone before my other support networks fail me, I only hope I have the financial capabilities to pay for proper care. I surely hope my well being never becomes placed in the hands of any government agency, where people are practically hired off the street and are about as reliable.

As I continue to go down the road that is my life, I also have to continually deal with death. I have been aware of suffering through disease, and death, from a very young age, and each year I am reminded when another friend of mine passes away. Sometimes I feel like I am an old woman, and the people I have known throughout my life are passing on, my turn soon to follow. People I know with disabilities similar to my own die every year, and sometimes I can't help to think that I might be next. I am only twenty years old.

My views about the future are also largely influenced by what I see in other people who have disabilities. My friend Angela has been such a wonderful person to know, we have spent our lives growing up together, comparing stories about the similar experiences we face. Being a few years older than me, I was able to go to her when I was unsure about college attendant care; it was she who we called when my wheelchair broke on the cruise; and it is she who has so many times given me the confidence to do things I may not have done had I not seen her do it first.

As we get older though, it is scary to see the phases she is approaching in her life. She recently graduated from college and is now working as a third grade teacher. Her students love her and are learning invaluable life lessons just by having her in their lives. Although she has such a wonderful career, it is a little disconcerting when she has had to move back home at times for lack of attendant care. Will we always be able to find help? What will happen when our parents are no longer able to bail us out?

There is a group I meet with every other week to talk about different issues we, as people with disabilities, face. The evening we discussed relationships I went home depressed. One of the people in the group is thirty years old and single, hoping to find a husband in the second round, picking through the divorcees. Will that be me?

So far in my life I have been well taken care of. I will just have to continue to take one day at a time...mustn't we all?

Epilogue

During my last year of college, I decided to go to law school. I applied and was accepted to almost every school in Texas, although many of them were not as prestigious as I would have liked. However, I was once again feeling limited in my options to travel due mostly to a lack of a support network in other states. I did decide, just for fun, to apply to Berkeley's law school, Boalt Hall. Wasn't I a bit blown away when I received an email one day informing me that I had been accepted!?! This changed everything. Suddenly there was a very real possibility that I would move far away from my parents and would have to start all over...accessible housing, transportation, attendant care...you name it.

My parents and I flew to Berkeley to visit the school. It was amazing. From the top of the road near the entrance of the law school you could look down and see the Bay. At the age of 22, the culture was richer than I had ever seen before. The subway system was completely accessible and afforded me much independence. I even met with other students who had disabilities and they all assured me that Berkeley was the best place you could live with a disability and that attendant care was of no concern. There was proof of this...everywhere I went there were wheelchairs. People didn't even flinch, no one turned to stare, because disability was so prevalent there. To add to the many benefits, my college roommate, Ashley, had been accepted to a graduate program in her field at Berkeley and though she would be unable to commit the time to be my only attendant, she

185

agreed to help out. I wouldn't be completely alone there. She could be my backup.

It was then that I started seriously considering the opportunity. There were a few dilemmas though. For instance, if I left my van in Texas, I would have no transportation other than the subway and/or buses in California. This would mean trips to the wine country would not be possible, rides to the airport would be difficult, appointments with the doctor or unexpected trips to the hospital would be hard. I would be very trapped. On the other hand, if I took my van to California, when I came home for holidays I would have no transportation. I would not even be able to get from the airport to my parents house without a $75 cab ride, and then I would be stuck at their house.

Secondly, what about the cost of education? I knew that I would be over $100,000 in debt if I went to school at Berkeley, yet I was interested in public interest law, a low paying career.

I had also heard the rumors about how difficult it is to find housing in Berkeley, and how expensive it is. I began to search for housing when I was there, and I saw first hand how true it was. Not only would I need a place to live, I needed something accessible...in a city filled with people with disabilities. Not many vacancies in that department.

Another concern was the weather. While 95% of the population would proclaim the weather there is perfect, I was freezing in April and knew I would miss the ninety degree days of Texas.

Even with all of this said, it was the hardest decision I have had to make thus far in my life. It is a very strange feeling to know that your entire future will be altered by one decision. The law school I would select would not only be determinative of my immediate experiences in the next years of my life, but my later financial situation, the opportunities offered to me after graduation, and even who I would meet and date and possibly spend the rest of my life with. Where was I meant to be? What path to take? I chose Austin.

In retrospect, I couldn't be happier with my decision. Maybe the reason I feel so content is because people need to believe that they make the right decisions; or maybe I was just really meant to stay here. I found a perfect apartment, my first. It was a quick walk to downtown Austin and in a great part of the city. I moved in with two girls who both assisted me. One of them, Randi, I met as an undergraduate, and I could not have been blessed with a more giving, compassionate, nurturing friend and caregiver. The other girl lived with us for a year, but moved out when Ashley called me to tell me she was moving back to Austin. I was thrilled. I couldn't imagine a better living situation than having two amazing people who were both familiar with my needs and who had seemingly worked them into their own lives in a way that maximized a physically, emotionally, and financially mutual beneficial situation.

My undergraduate education ended with a bang. A professor of history I had, Dr. Miller, nominated me for the Mike Wacker Award and I was chosen as the recipient. Not only did I get a lifetime membership to the Texas Exes, but I was recognized on the 50 yard line at a UT football game (which UT fans know are a HUGE deal!). I also successfully completed a thesis in psychology, which examined the perceptions the general public has of people with physical disabilities. I graduated in December of 2001 with highest honors and departmental honors.

Professionally, I had some great accomplishments at a young age. I was selected as the only Texas representative to participate in a two-week legislative training in Washington, D.C. concerning issues related to people with disabilities. There I attended training sessions led by the main author of the Americans with Disabilities Act. My childhood friend Stacey and I are still friends, and she went with me as my attendant.

After the training, we rented a van with a lift and drove to New York. Neither one of us had ever been. Not only did I get to meet the author of the ADA that week, but after I was lifted inside by a few strange men, I was also able to take a picture with Rupert of the Hello Deli (Dave Letterman fans know what I am referring to!).

I was also named Employee of the Year by the Austin Mayor's Committee on People with Disabilities for the work I did at the Coalition of Texans with Disabilities. My work at CTD consisted primarily of advocating bills in the legislative session, including drafting bills, testifying at bill hearings, and meeting individually with legislative staff. I also wrote a grant application, which we were awarded. I was then responsible for the project, which was to research and help write the Biennial Report to the Texas Legislature on personal assistance services for people with disabilities.

After my first year in law school I did an internship at the Texas Civil Rights Project, which was an amazing learning experience and my first encounter with the legal world of pleadings and discovery. The following summer and fall I worked at a prestigious plaintiff's firm in Austin and further sharpened my legal writing and research skills.

The past few years have not just been a time for me to build a resume though. I have also become more willing to take risks than I was before. In March, after I graduated, I decided that after four years of my best friend living in California, it was time for me to go visit her. My dad took me to the airport, put me on the plane, and I flew alone for the first time. It was a bit strange to think I couldn't get up from that seat if I wanted to and there was no one who would feel particularly obligated to assist me, but it was invigorating nonetheless. I knew that I was going to fall forward when the plane landed so I just asked the woman next to me if she would mind holding me up. She did great.

190

Lauren met me at the plane in Los Angeles and lifted me from my seat to my wheelchair. I was pleasantly surprised to discover that the airlines didn't even break my wheelchair. I had arranged a rental van with a lift and Lauren had asked the maintenance people at her apartment to install a homemade handheld shower for her bathtub. It consisted of a huge plastic tube and a lot of duct tape. It got me clean. We also purchased a "shower chair" at Target; in the patio section.

We had such an amazing week. It was so nice to be able to meet her friends, whom I had heard about for years, to see where she lived, and to be able to just sit around and do nothing together. Unfortunately, the day before I was to fly home our rental van was towed! It took eleven hours and two hundred dollars to get it back. For a few hours there I wasn't sure how I was going to get back to the airport!

That summer the Muscular Dystrophy Association asked me to return to the camp where I had graduated the year before in order to be a speaker to the older campers. Knowing so many of the campers, and knowing that so many of their parents were not as supportive as mine and were sheltering them beyond belief, I took the opportunity to tell them, first hand, how many options were open to them. I told them about my adventure flying alone across the country…I told them it isn't a big deal, just get someone to put you on the plane…but be sure there is someone there waiting for you on the other end! The campers and the attendants had a ton of questions about college and life away from home. I think it was really good for them to hear what I had to say and it was good for me too. I was able to get the closure I wasn't ready for the year before when I was "forced" to graduate due to my age. That afternoon I ate with the campers, went to their dance, and realized that I felt really ready for that chapter of my life to be over. I was moving on to bigger and better things.

Law school certainly offered that. For the first time in my life I was living on my own, making a future for myself, and feeling more confident than ever. Nothing could have been better. But wait…what about my love life? I think if we are honest with ourselves, as successful as we may be and as wonderful as our friends and family may be, true happiness is hard to come by if there is no one to share your life with. I think it probably took me a little longer than usual to really feel comfortable with the idea of being with someone. Sure I often had crushes on guys, but…well let's just say I cringed and felt nauseated when someone expressed interest in me. I wasn't ready for that. I had done good to feel comfortable getting naked in the community shower in the dorms, but to have a man undress me?! I couldn't even conceptualize how I would end up having a sexual experience with someone who would later have to put me on the toilet. It is so interesting how the people that you meet and the interactions that you have help you to grow and become ready for the next adventures in life. Of course I wasn't ready. I couldn't go from being completely sexually inexperienced without a love interest in my life to being completely intimate with a man in one night. Not my style,

192

and not with the physical help I would need for that to become a reality.

The difficult part is finding someone you want to make it a reality with. When you are in school, meeting new people your age all the time, you become aware of how rare it is to meet someone that you really feel connected to. It isn't about having things in common, or being conversationally compatible, or even thinking someone is physically attractive; it is about a feeling that comes over you. It is about a desire to know that person more. It is about not feeling ashamed or embarrassed about who you are and what your needs are. It is rare, and it is wonderful.

I have always been haunted by the idea: could a beautiful, intelligent, charming man be attracted to me? After my first year in law school, I had my answer. Some people just get it, and I met someone who got it. Someone who didn't see me as a wheelchair, bur rather an intelligent, sexy young woman. Although the circumstances were not quite right (after all, timing is everything!), I think he was put into my life to build my confidence. To give me hope for the future. To give me the realization that I am ready.

So what about today? I have graduated from law school and taken the bar exam. I am still having nightmares about that horrible 3-day test which is in reality a form of hazing for those hoping to ascertain the title of "lawyer." While I admit that I learned more about the law in the two months that preceded the Bar Exam than I did the entire time in law school, I also found the process to be such a waste of time and energy. I wonder who came up with the idea of making us memorize and spit back an unfathomable amount of information, which we will never again have to recall from memory (thanks to law books and the internet!). At least it is over.

The first half of my "twenties" has taught me something very important about myself: I am constantly seeking new adventures, challenges, and life experiences. This undoubtedly has to do with the views on life that I've developed through exposure to disability and death while I was growing up. For this reason, while being an attorney is great for now, who knows what I will be doing in 10 years.

Another major change that has occurred in the past year was my moving into an apartment alone. Yes, that is right, I live alone! Five years ago I would have said it was impossible, but it has worked out wonderfully. Like many young adults, I got so tired of dealing with roommates. I was annoyed by the filth, the lack of privacy, the drama, and I was especially tired of living with my attendants who inevitably would become too comfortable with me as a roommate, resulting in substandard quality of care as an attendant. So I put up an ad in the paper and hired several people. A few of them alternate evenings and stay with me during the night. They arrive at 10 or 11pm, assist me in getting ready for bed, sleep at my apartment, and then help me in the morning. The others meet me periodically throughout the day, both at home and work, to assist me in using the restroom. In addition, there are often times when I am between attendants or someone becomes unavailable, and my dad has to help out. For the past several weeks, he has been meeting me every single day around lunchtime to help me with the restroom. On top of that, a few years ago my mom injured her back and has not been able to lift me ever since. So each day I spend time making calls and planning my bathrooms breaks…who can help today and at what times? I have to schedule my social life around when my attendants can meet me to use the restroom too. I love spending time with friends who are strong enough to lift me because it is the one time I can just be, without having to worry about how and when I will be able to go to the restroom next time. It is exhausting. There is also a lot of turnover with attendants because it is low paying part time work and people are continually moving forward. This means I am constantly running ads, interviewing, training, scheduling, and starting all over. It is a huge burden that will always be a part of my life, BUT it means I can live an independent life, which couldn't be more worth it.

Not only am I living alone, but I have also been exploring another facet of independence, travel. Thus far, I have been pleasantly surprised with how feasible it is. Although I have always desired to visit other parts of the world, I never thought it was much of an option for me. And while it is true that I will never be able to travel totally alone; with the right travel companion, the possibilities are endless.

When my childhood friend, Lauren, finished her undergraduate education in California, she moved to Hawaii to get a master's degree in environmental engineering. After living there for two years, Lauren called me and said, "if you want to come visit me in Hawaii, you should come soon because I am moving when I graduate." How could I not go? But I would need a travel companion.

I met Michael at a coffee shop in Austin. He approached me one afternoon when I was in my second year of law school and asked me if I had gone to Sundown Elementary. That's what happens when you are the only kid in a wheelchair - your peers remember you 15 years later. Well, a conversation or two and approximately 500 cups of coffee later, Michael was accompanying me to Hawaii. He had already assisted me in using the restroom, so I knew he was strong. I also knew how much strength it would take to get me to Hawaii. My main concerns were the eight-hour flight and the miniature restrooms provided on the plane. In fact, when I first proposed the trip to Michael, I warned him, "I will have to use the restroom on the plane and it isn't going to be easy. Not only will it be hard, but you will have to carry me down the aisle and everyone will be staring." Well I was right, at least partially. It was hard, but I honestly didn't notice if people were staring. I suppose that is a sign of being really comfortable with someone.

We had such an amazing time. Michael assisted me with most of my personal care, and where he left off, Lauren was able to step in. We rented a van with a lift so we were able to see all of Oahu, including many beaches where they provided a free "beach wheelchair." The beach wheelchair had huge tires that maneuvered easily over the sand, and it actually floated, so we pushed it right into the ocean. I made sure to lie on the beach and when in the water I got out of the chair into the ocean too. I hadn't been in an ocean since I was about 8 years old! Hawaii was just the beginning though. I am traveling to Europe with my parents and a friend soon, and next on the list is Peru. I know that, for myself, experiencing different parts of the world is key to leading a fulfilled life, despite the extra challenges I have in attaining those experiences.

I want to end this book with one last anecdote, a sobering reality that was recently brought to my attention. A woman who handles my case file was telling me that I would be a prime candidate for a nursing home because of the level of assistance I need. Further, she told me that I am very spoiled in the way I have become accustomed to living (i.e. frequency of using the restroom, which is usually 4 times a day). I need thousands and thousands of dollars worth of help per year, albeit underpaid, just to live my life. If I am able to make $40,000 per year in salary and not rely on my parents for emergency help, grocery shopping etc., it will cost me $20,000 in out of pocket attendant care. Therefore, it seems impossible to get ahead, to be self-sufficient, and to live a lifestyle outside of poverty if you have a disability. And if you can get the government to help defray these costs, you have to hide the truth so they won't hide you away. While the woman was very understanding and helpful, she was also candid regarding the state agencies and the politicians that determine availability of benefits to people with disabilities. With the arbitrary and unrealistic rules and regulations we have to abide by, the bottom line is: they don't care enough for it to matter.

I want everyone who has just read this book to know that I "belong in a nursing home." I am twenty-six years old, I have a law degree, I have written a book, I am dating, I live alone in a loft apartment in downtown Austin, I frequent happy hours, I travel; but I belong in a nursing home. If you have ever visited a nursing home you know that they smell of urine; people are screaming, crying, and rambling; the food is disgusting; your life is limited to a television set and the four walls that form your shared room; and you are nothing but a patient to all those who interact with you on a daily basis. This is not an appropriate atmosphere for me or for anyone with a mere disability. Please remember my story.

Other Books

Books from Science & Humanities Press

Disabilities and Adaptation

HOW TO TRAVEL—A Guidebook for Persons with a Disability – Fred Rosen (1997) ISBN 1-888725-05-2, 5½ X 8¼, 120 pp, $9.95 **18-point large print edition** (1998) ISBN 1-888725-17-6 7X8, 120 pp, $19.95

HOW TO TRAVEL in Canada—A Guidebook for A Visitor with a Disability – Fred Rosen (2000) ISBN 1-888725-26-5, 5½X8¼, 180 pp, $14.95 **MacroPrintBooks™ edition** (2001) ISBN 1-888725-30-3 7X8, 16 pt, 200 pp, $19.95

How to travel to and in Britain & Northern Ireland : a guidebook for visitors with a disability – Fred Rosen (2006) ISBN 1-888725-47-8, 5½X8¼, 190 pp, $14.95 **MacroPrintBooks™ edition** (2001) ISBN 1-888725-48-6, 7X8, 16 pt, 200 pp, $19.95

AVOIDING Attendants from HELL: A Practical Guide to Finding, Hiring & Keeping Personal Care Attendants 2nd Edn—June Price, (2002), accessible plastic spiral bind, ISBN 1-888725-72-9 8¼X10½, 125 pp, $16.95, School/library edition (2002) ISBN 1-888725-60-5, 8¼X6½, 200 pp, $18.95

Sometimes MS is Yucky Kimberly Harrold, Illustrated by Eric Whitfield (2005) Illustrated color booklet for children ages 3-8 who have a parent or loved one with Multiple Sclerosis Includes a "Parent Section" with suggestions on therapeutic activities for providing emotional support to kids dealing with MS in their young lives ISBN 1-59630-006-X Thirty two pp $7.95

I Like to Run Too—Two decades of sitting—A memoir of growing up with a physical disability. Stacy Zoern (2006) The extraordinary accomplishments of young Stacy Zoern, who was born with a disability but adapted to become an attorney and business owner before age 30. ISBN 1-59630-017-5, 5½X8¼, 200 pp. extensively illustrated. $16.95

Biography

Virginia Mayo—The Best Years of My Life (2002) Autobiography of film star Virginia Mayo as told to LC Van Savage. From her early days in Vaudeville and the Muny in St Louis to the dozens of hit motion pictures, with dozens of photographs. ISBN 1-888725-53-2, 5½ X 8¼, 200 pp, $16.95

To Norma Jeane With Love, Jimmie -Jim Dougherty as told to LC Van Savage (2001) ISBN 1-888725-51-6 The sensitive and touching story of Jim Dougherty's teenage bride who later became Marilyn Monroe. Dozens of photographs. "The Marilyn Monroe book of the year!" As seen on TV. 5½X8¼, 200 pp, $16.95 **MacroPrintBooks™ edition** ISBN 1-888725-52-4, 8¼X6½, 16 pt, 290pp, $24.95

Ropes and Saddles—Andy Polson (2001) Cowboy (and other) poems by Andy Polson. Reminiscences of the Wyoming poet. ISBN 1-888725-39-7, 5½ X 8¼, 100 pp, $9.95 **MacroPrintBooks™ edition (2006)** ISBN 1-59630-018-3 8¼ X 11, 16 pt $19.95

Ellos Pasaron por Aqui — 99 New Mexicans and a Few Other Folks (2005) compilation of old-time stories illustrates how the Wild West really was during New Mexico's frontier era. ISBN 1-888725-92-3, 6½ X 8¼, 350 pp, $16.95 **MacroPrintBooks™ edition** ISBN 1-888725-93-1, 350pp 8¼ X 11, 16 pt, $24.95

Bloodville — Don Bullis (2002) Fictional adaptation of the Budville, NM murders by New Mexico crime historian, Don Bullis. 5½ X 8¼, 350 pp ISBN: 1-888725-75-3 $14.95 **MacroPrintBooks™ edition** (2003) 16 pt. 8¼X11 460pp ISBN: 1-888725-76-1 $24.95

Serious thought and just for fun

Spiritual Journeys in Prayer and Song with music CD, Reverend Peter Unger, 2006. Short Christian meditations with accompanying songs on CD ISBN 1-59630-009-4 (regular print edition) 5½X8¼, 185 pp, $24.95 ISBN 1-59630-010-8 **MacroPrintBooks** Large Print edition, 16 point type $29.95

The Bridge Never Crossed—A Survivor's Search for Meaning. Captain George A. Burk (1999) The inspiring story of George Burk, lone survivor of a military{ XE "military" } plane crash, who overcame extensive burn injuries to earn a presidential award and become a highly successful motivational speaker. ISBN 1-888725-16-8, 5½X8¼, 170 pp, illustrated. $16.95 **MacroPrintBooks™ Edition** (1999) ISBN 1-888725-28-1 $24.95

Value Centered Leadership—A Survivor's Strategy for Personal and Professional Growth—Captain George A. Burk (2004) Principles of Leadership & Total Quality Management applied to all aspects of living. ISBN 1-888725-59-1, 5½X8¼, 120 pp, $16.95

Plague Legends: from the Miasmas of Hippocrates to the Microbes of Pasteur-Socrates Litsios D.Sc. (2001) Medical progress from early history through the 19th Century in understanding origins and spread of contagious disease. A thorough but readable and enlightening history of medicine. Illustrated, Bibliography, Index ISBN 1-888725-33-8, 6¼X8¼, 250pp, $24.95

Republican or Democrat? (2005) Moses Sanchez, who describes himself as "a Black Hispanic" thinks for himself, questions the stereotypes, examines the facts and makes his own decision. Early Editions Books ISBN 1-888725-32-X 5½X8¼, 176pp pp, $14.95

The Stress Myth -Serge Doublet, PhD (2000) A thorough examination of the concept that 'stress' is the source of unexplained afflictions. Debunking mysticism, psychologist Serge Doublet reviews the history of other concepts such as 'demons', 'humors', 'hysteria' and 'neurasthenia' that had been placed in this role in the past, and provides an alternative approach for more success in coping with life's challenges. ISBN 1-888725-36-2, 5½X8¼, 280 pp, $24.95

Me and My Shadows—Shadow Puppet Fun for Kids of All Ages—Elizabeth Adams, Revised Edition by Dr. Bud Banis (2000) A thoroughly illustrated guide to the art of shadow puppet entertainment using tools that are always at hand wherever you go. A perfect gift for children and adults. ISBN 1-888725-44-3, 7X8¼, 67 pp, 12.95
MacroPrintBooks™ edition (2002) ISBN 1-888725-78-8 8½X11 lay-flat spiral, 18 pt, 67 pp, $16.95

Journey to a Closed City with the International Executive Service Corps—Russell R. Miller (2004) ISBN 1-888725-94-X, Describes the adventures of a retired executive volunteering with the senior citizens' equivalent of the Peace Corp as he applies his professional skills in a former Iron Curtain city emerging into the dawn of a new economy.This book is essential reading for anyone approaching retirement who is interested in opportunities to exercise skills to "do good" during expense-paid travel to intriguing locations. Journey to A Closed City should also appeal to armchair travelers eager to explore far-off corners of the world in our rapidly-evolving global community. paperback,
5½X8¼,270pp,$16.95 **MacroPrintBooks™ edition** (2004) ISBN 1-888725-94-8, 8¼X6½, 18 pt, 150 pp, $24.95

50 Things You Didn't Learn in School–But Should Have: Little known facts that still affect our world today (2005) by John Naese, . ISBN 1-888725-49-4, 5½X8¼, 200 pp, illustrated. $16.95

Inaugural Addresses: Presidents of the United States from George Washington to 2008 -3rd Edition– Robert J. Banis, PhD, CMA, Ed. (2005) ISBN 1-59630-004-3, 7X8½, 400pp., extensively illustrated, includes election statistics, Vice-presidents, principal opponents, coupons for update supplements for the upcoming election $18.95

Sexually Transmitted Diseases—Symptoms, Diagnosis, Treatment, Prevention-2nd Edition – NIAID Staff, Assembled and Edited by R.J.Banis, PhD, (2006) Teacher friendly —free to copy for education. Illustrated with more than 70 figures and photographs of lesions, ISBN 1-888725-58-3, 8¼X5½, 290 pp, $18.95

Youth Risk Behavior Survey with Student Guide for Statistical Analysis in EXCEL, R. J. Banis, PhD & Centers for Disease Control Staff (2006) ISBN 1-888725-24-9 Heuristic Books, 8½X11, spiral bound, 250 pp, $28.95

Large Print Classics

Paul the Peddler or The Fortunes of a Young Street Merchant—Horatio Alger, jr A Classic reprinted in accessible large type, (1998 **MacroPrintBooks**™ reprint in 24-point type) ISBN 1-888725-02-8, 8¼X10½, 276 pp, $16.95

The Wisdom of Father Brown—G.K. Chesterton (2000) A Classic collection of detective stories reprinted in accessible 22-point type ISBN 1-888725-27-3 8¼X10½, 276 pp, $18.95

Buttered Side Down—Short Stories by Edna Ferber (BeachHouse Books reprint 2000) A classic collection of stories by the beloved author of Showboat, Giant, and Cimarron. ISBN 1-888725-43-5, 5½X8¼, 190 pp, $12.95 **MacroPrintBooks**™ **Edition** (2000) ISBN 1-888725-40-0 7X8¼,16 pt, 240 pp $18.95

The Four Million: The Gift of the Magi & other favorites. Life in New York City around 1900—O. Henry. **MacroPrintBooks™ edition** (2001) ISBN 1-888725-41-9 7X8¼, 16 pt, 270 pp $18.95; ISBN 1-888725-03-6, 8¼X10½, 22 pt, 300pp, $22.95

Bar-20: Hopalong Cassidy's Rustler Roundup— Clarence Mulford (reprint 2000). Classical Western Tale. Not the TV version. ISBN 1-888725-34-6 5½X8¼, 223 pp, $12.95 **MacroPrintBooks™ edition** ISBN 1-888725-42-7, 8¼X6½, 16 pt, 385pp, $18.95

Contemporary Fiction (available in large print)

The Gift of the Magic -and other enchanting character-building stories for smart teenage girls who want to grow up to be strong women. Richard Showstack, (2004) 1-888725-64-8 5½ X8¼, 145 pp, $14.95 **MacroPrintBooks™** edition ISBN 1-888725-65-8¼X6½, 16 pt, 280 pp, $24.95

A Horse Named Peggy-and other enchanting character-building stories for smart teenage boys who want to grow up to be good men. Richard Showstack, (2004) 1-888725-66-4. 5½ X8¼, 145 pp, $14.95 **MacroPrintBooks™** edition ISBN 1-888725-67, 8¼X6½, 16 pt, 280 pp, $24.95

Nursing Home – Ira Eaton, PhD, (1997) You will be moved and disturbed by this novel. ISBN 1-888725-01-X, 5½X8¼, 300 pp, $12.95 **MacroPrintBooks™ edition** (1999) ISBN 1-888725-23-0,8¼X10½, 16 pt, 330 pp, $18.95

The Job—Eric Whitfield (2001) A story of self-discovery in the context of the death of a grandfather.. A book to read and share in times of change and Grieving. ISBN 1-888725-68-0, 5½ X 8¼, 100 pp, $12.95 **MacroPrintBooks™ edition** (2001) ISBN 1-888725-69-9, 8¼X6½, 18 pt, 150 pp, $18.95

The Cut—John Evans (2003). Football, Mystery and Mayhem in a highschool setting by John Evans ISBN: 1-888725-82-6 5½ X 8¼, 100 pp $14.95 **MacroPrintBooks**™ edition (2003) 16 pt. ISBN: 1-888725-83-4 $24.95

MamaSquad! (2001) Hilarious novel by Clarence Wall about what happens when a group of women from a retirement home get tangled up in Army Special Forces. ISBN 1-888725-13-3 5½ X8¼, 200 pp, $14.95 **MacroPrintBooks**™ **edition** (2001) ISBN 1-888725-14-1 8¼X6½ 16 pt, 300 pp, $24.95

Tales from the Woods of Wisdom—(book I)— Richard Tichenor (2000) In a spirit someplace between The Wizard of Oz and The Celestine Prophecy, this is more than a childrens' fable of life in the deep woods. ISBN 1-888725-37-0, 5½X8¼, 185 pp, $16.95 **MacroPrintBooks**™ **edition** (2001) ISBN 1-888725-50-8 6X8¼, 16 pt, 270 pp $24.95

Rhythm of the Sea —Shari Cohen (2001). Delightful collection of heartwarming stories of life relationships set in the context of oceans and lakes. Shari Cohen is a popular author of Womens' magazine articles and contributor to the Chicken Soup for the Soul series. ISBN 1-888725-55-9, 8X6.5 150 pp, $14.95 **MacroPrintBooks**™ **edition** (2001) ISBN 1-888725-63-X, 8¼X6½, 16 pt, 250 pp, $24.95

Riverdale Chronicles—Charles F. Rechlin (2003). Life, living and character studies in the setting of the Riverdale Golf Club by Charles F. Rechlin 5½ X 8¼, 100 pp ISBN: 1-888725-84-2 $14.95 **MacroPrintBooks**™ edition (2003) 16 pt. 8¼X6½, 16 pt, 350 pp ISBN: 1-888725-85-0 $24.95

Winners and Losers--Charles F. Rechlin (2005). a collection of humorous short stories portraying misadventures of attorneys, stock brokers, and others in the Urban workplace.ISBN 1-59630-002-7 BeachHouse Books Edition $14.95 ISBN 1-59630-003-5 **MacroPrintBooks Edition** (large print) $24.95

Perfect Love-A Novel by Mary Harvatich (2000) Love born in an orphanage endures ISBN 1-888725-29-X 5½X8¼, 200 pp, $12.95 MacroPrintBooks™ edition (2000) ISBN 1-888725-15-X, 8¼X10½, 16 pt, 200 pp, $18.95

The Way It Was

Nostalgic Tales of HotRods and Romance

Chuck Klein

The Way It Was-- Nostalgic Tales of Hotrods and Romance Chuck Klein (2003) Series of hotrod stories by author of Circa 1957 in collaboration with noted illustrator Bill Lutz BeachHouse Books edition 5½ X 8¼, 200 pp ISBN: 1-888725-86-9 $14.95 **MacroPrintBooks**™ edition (2003) 16 pt. 8¼X6½, 350pp ISBN: 1-888725-87-7 $24.95

Lure of the Long-Legged Blond--Norman Mark (2005) A rollicking ride featuring a lovable, intellectually-challenged loser. An hysterical parody of detective tales for mature readers. ISBN 1-888725-57-5, 5½ X 8¼, 188 pp $14.95

Science & Humanities Press

Publishes fine books under the imprints:

- Science & Humanities Press
- BeachHouse Books
- MacroPrint Books
- Heuristic Books
- Early Editions Books

Route 66 books by Michael Lund

Growing Up on Route 66 —Michael Lund (2000) ISBN 1-888725-31-1 Novel evoking fond memories of what it was like to grow up alongside "America's Highway" in 20th Century Missouri. (Trade paperback) 5½ X8¼, 260 pp, $14.95 **MacroPrintBooks**™ edition (2001) ISBN 1-888725-45-1 8¼X6½, 16 pt, 330 pp, $24.95. **AudioBook** on CD— Growing Up on Route 66 ISBN: 1-59630-021-3 by Michael Lund abridged 6 CD's --7 Hours running time. $24.95

Route 66 Kids —Michael Lund (2002) ISBN 1-888725-70-2 Sequel to *Growing Up on Route 66*, continuing memories of what it was like to grow up alongside "America's Highway" in 20th Century Missouri. (Trade paperback) 5½ X8¼, 270 pp, $14.95 **MacroPrintBooks**™ edition (2002) ISBN 1-888725-71-0 8¼X6½, 16 pt, 350 pp, $24.95

Route 66 Spring-- Michael Lund (2004) ISBN: 1-888725-98-2. The lives of four young Missourians are changed when a bottle comes to the surface of one of the state's many natural springs. Inside is a letter written by a girl a dozen years after the end of the Civil War. Lucy Rivers Johns ' epistle contains a sad story of family failure and a powerful plea for help. This message from the last century crystallizes the individual frustrations of Janet Masters, Freddy Sills, Louis Clark, and Roberta Green, another group of Route 66 kids. Their response to the past charts a bold path into the future, a path inspired by the Mother Road itself. (Trade paperback) 5½ X8¼, 270 pp, $14.95. **MacroPrintBooks™ edition** (2002) ISBN 1-888725-99-0. 8¼X6½, 16 pt, 350 pp, $24.95.

A Left-hander on Route 66--Michael Lund (2003) ISBN 1-888725-88-5. Twenty years after the fact, left-hander Hugh Noone appeals a wrongful conviction that detoured him from "America's Main Street" and put him in jail. But revealing the details of the past and effecting a resolution of his case mean a dramatic rearrangement of his world, including troubled relationships with three women: Linda Roy, Patty Simpson, and Karen Murphy. (Trade paperback) 5½ X8¼, 270 pp, $14.95 **MacroPrintBooks**™ edition (2002) ISBN 1-888725-89-3 8¼X6½, 16 pt, 350 pp, $24.95

Miss Route 66--Michael Lund (2004) ISBN 1-888725-96-6. In the fourth novel of Michael Lund's Route 66 Novel Series, Susan Bell tells the story of her candidacy in Fairfield, Missouri's annual beauty contest. Now married and with teenage children in St. Louis, she recounts her youthful adventure in this small town along "America's Highway." At the same time, she plans a return to Fairfield in order to right injustices she feels were done to some young contestants in the Miss Route 66 Pageant. (Trade paperback) 5½ X8¼, 260 pp, $14.95 **MacroPrintBooks**™ edition (2004) ISBN 1-888725-97-4 8¼X6½, 16 pt, 350 pp, $24.95 **Audiobook** on 5 CD's ISBN 1-888725-12-5 $24.95

Route 66 to Vietnam Michael Lund (2004) ISBN 1-59630-000-0 This novel takes characters from earlier works in the Route 66 Novel Series farther west than Los Angeles, official destination of the famous highway, Route 66. Mark Landon and Billy Rhodes find the values they grew up on challenged by America's role in Southeast Asia. But elements of their upbringing represented by the Mother Road also sustain them in ways they could never have anticipated. . (Trade paperback) 5½ X8¼, 270 pp, $14.95. **MacroPrintBooks**™ **edition** (2004) ISBN 1-59630-001-9. 8¼X6½, 16 pt, 350 pp, $24.95.

AudioBook on 6 CD's ISBN: 1-59630-011-6 Michael Lund's fictional commentary from the viewpoint of a draftee. by Michael Lund unabridged 6 CD's --9 hours running time. $24.95

Route 66 Chapel Michael Lund (2006) ISBN 1-59630-012-4
Route 66 Chapel, Michael Lund (2006) (Trade paperback)
5½ X8¼, 260 pp, $14.95. When the forces of progress
threaten the foundation of smalltown life—a small church—
five senior citizens, a mysterious newcomer, and one young
couple band together in an unlikely campaign to save it. The
embattled meeting point of old and new is Route 66 Chapel,
a building curiously linked to America's "Mother Road."
MacroPrintBooks™ edition ISBN 1-59630-013-2,. 8¼X6½,
16 pt, 340 pp, $24.95.

Educators Discount Policy

To encourage use of our books for education, educators can
purchase three or more books (mixed titles) on our standard
discount schedule for resellers. See
**sciencehumanitiespress.com/educator/
educator.html** for more detail or call

Science & Humanities Press, PO Box 7151,

Chesterfield MO 63006-7151 636-394-4950

Our books are guaranteed:

If a book has a defect, or doesn't hold up under
normal use, or if you are unhappy in any way
with one of our books, we are interested to know
about it and will replace it and credit reasonable
return shipping costs. Products with publisher
defects (i.e., books with missing pages, etc.) may
be returned at any time without authorization.
However, we request that you describe the
problem, to help us to continuously improve.

I Like to Run Too—Two decades of sitting—A memoir of growing up with a physical disability. Stacy Zoern (2006) The extraordinary accomplishments of young Stacy Zoern, who was born with a disability but adapted to become an attorney and business owner before age 30. ISBN 1-59630-017-5, 5½X8¼, 200 pp. extensively illustrated. $16.95

Order Form

Item	Each	Quantity	Amount
Missouri (only) sales tax 6.075%			
Priority Shipping			$5.00
	Total		
Name			
Address			

Science & Humanities Press

PO Box 7151

Chesterfield, MO 63006-7151

(636) 394-4950
sciencehumanitiespress.com